The Practitioner Inqui

D0198062

Marilyn Cochran-Smith and Susan L.

(continued)

TEACHING AS INQUIRY

Asking Hard Questions to Improve Practice and Student Achievement

ALEXANDRA WEINBAUM
DAVID ALLEN
TINA BLYTHE
KATHERINE SIMON
STEVE SEIDEL
CATHERINE RUBIN

Teachers College
Columbia University
New York and London

National Staff
Development Council
Oxford, Ohio

Published simultaneously by Teachers College Press, 1234 Amsterdam Avenue, New York, NY 10027 and by the National Staff Development Council, P.O. Box 240, Oxford, OH 45056

Library of Congress Cataloging-in-Publication Data

Teaching as inquiry : asking hard questions to improve practice and student achievement / Alexandra Weinbaum . . . [et al.].
    p. cm. — (The practitioner inquiry series)
  Includes bibliographical references and index.
  ISBN 0-8077-4458-1 (cloth : alk. paper) — ISBN 0-8077-4457-3 (pbk. : alk. paper)
    1. Educational evaluation—United States—Case studies.   2. Group work in education—United States—Case studies.   I. Weinbaum, Alexandra.
II. Series.
  LB2822.75.Q37   2004
  371.2'03—dc22   2003068737

ISBN 0-8077-4457-3 (paper)
ISBN 0-8077-4458-1 (cloth)

Printed on acid-free paper
Manufactured in the United States of America

11 10 09 08 07 06 05 04   8 7 6 5 4 3 2 1

To our colleague, Nancy Mohr,
whose dedication to collaboration
inspired us and educators across the country.

Contents

6. Engaging Equity and District Mandates: Inquiry at Melrose Elementary School   122

Tom Malarkey

PART III:
TOWARD A CULTURE OF INQUIRY

7. Milestones and Discoveries: A Cross-Case Commentary   141

8. Toward a Culture of Inquiry: Reflections and Policy Implications   146

Foreword

Most people who work with educational reform projects soon discover that the facilitators of the reform are learners, too, not only of the process of implementing the reform but of its content. Trying to figure out how to share those learnings with an audience beyond the project led the Wallace Foundation to decide to fund a National Study Group (NSG), comprised of the Academy of Educational Development in New York City, the Coalition of Essential Schools, and Project Zero, all of which were working with teachers who were engaged in collaborative inquiry about student work as a means of improving their practice and student learning. We played the role of outsiders, critical friends of the project, who were interested in the idea of collaborative inquiry into student work and its role in the improvement of teaching practice and student learning. The National Study Group became the forum for collaborative inquiry and mutual learning across the three organizations, where they built on each other's work, thus expanding the individual learning of projects to collective learning.

The big idea was for the project participants to discuss their work, identify their problems and challenges, and engage in inquiry on their roles and experiences supporting teachers' learning about their practice through the examination of their students' work. Meeting twice a year, the National Study Group facilitated a cross-organization conversation in which each member, with the help of the others and the critical friends, could test out the group's ideas; analyze its experiences with teachers; discuss its puzzlements, dilemmas, progress, and successes; examine its assumptions; and obtain feedback and collegial support for the challenges that it would inevitably face.

DIFFERENT PERSPECTIVES, CONTEXTS, LANGUAGE, AND WAYS OF WORKING

Like any new group, the participants needed to develop relationships to define the work on which they would collaborate. And like most groups, finding the common ground was easier said than done. Even though the organizations had very compatible educational values and orientations and were presumably all doing the same thing, each was working in a different context—different parts of the country, different school levels, different community demographics, and different pedagogical commitments. Two of the projects had solid relationships with the schools and teachers, where they had been working for a while. One project was responding to a district-wide mandate to teach teachers to "look at student work." Each had very different reasons for doing the work and very different ways of engaging the teachers. These differences were to be expected. But because of the philosophical compatibility of the three organizations, what was not expected was their struggle to organize the conversation, to communicate, to construct a common language—to construct common meaning for their language—to build trust, and to ensure equal voice, all of which became manifest in the initial meetings. What would be the norms for the conversation? What would be the nature of the protocol for its conduct, especially since some members were averse to protocols while others had a history of relying on them? Initially, people talked past each other. Depending upon the project, the language had different meanings. And no matter how much each project tried to engage in productive dialogue, the different modes of work, the different contexts within which the projects resided, and the different cultural meanings and purposes of the projects presented obstacles and challenges to their engagement and communication with one another.

Desperately wanting these national gatherings to work, we collectively designed a task that we hoped would break the logjam. Each project agreed to bring a description of how they worked when they were successful with teachers. *Voilà!* There was a breakthrough! Each group spoke from its own understanding and context so that all the rest of us could see it, and each group modeled how it worked when it was doing well. This created a more trusting environment and began to establish a base of understanding that enabled the groups to frame more focused questions about their own work and to provide feedback to the other groups that was more connected to their context and purposes. In this manner the national conversation became more valuable and more pragmatically useful.

BUILDING A COLLABORATIVE CULTURE IN THE NATIONAL STUDY GROUP

As external "critical friends" we began to understand that this National Study Group that was expected to collaborate was not unlike other reform projects that we knew and had experienced. The first lesson is that people need to trust one another enough to talk about their work and make it public so that it can be understood by others. This became the first building block to a rich collaboration (one that we knew was an experience that all three projects facilitated in their work with others). As time went on the group examined questions and artifacts; debated issues of scaling up and sustainability; had discussions of voluntarism and compliance; and explored the tensions of ownership and partnerships. As critical friends, we shared our perspectives and questions on the process of their conversation as well as the content of their work, helping the group to interrogate and understand it. Over the period of 3 years, the NSG nurtured risk-taking and risk-taking nurtured trust. Conversation deepened as participants more deeply revealed their work and as others more deeply understood each other and each other's work and context more clearly and accurately.

Collaborative Inquiry in Schools

The engagement of the three organizations in their own collaborative inquiry in many ways mirrored the experience of the schools with which they worked. They capture that experience in their wonderful and insightful book that incisively and very thoughtfully investigates, describes, and analyzes the theoretical and practical landscape of collaborative inquiry and the experiences of the schools that they helped engage in collaborative inquiry. In an era of scripted curriculum and standardized tests that confuse test prep with education, this book makes a powerful argument for collaborative inquiry and the struggle for knowledge, the tolerance of ambiguity, and the quest for meaning that undergird it. Carefully connecting theory, research, and practice, the authors take us on a thorough and rigorous journey through the literature on collaborative inquiry as well as vivid case studies where we see teachers and schools actively engaged in collaborative inquiry.

Throughout, we see that teaching, like learning, is fundamentally an enduring struggle for meaning and inquiry is the catalyst in this struggle. We see the role of collaborative inquiry in creating a professional community where experts and novices learn together from the examination of cases and the support of effective practice. Together, members of inquiry groups hold themselves and their colleagues accountable by surfacing unexamined assumptions and conceptual constructs, the influence of which they analyze by reflecting on the mental models that shape the school as an organization and by asking and demanding answers to questions such as, Where are we going? How well are we doing? What have we learned from outside experts, other schools and teachers, and our own experiences? How can we support each other in improving our practice?

We learn what conditions are necessary for successful collaborative inquiry: relational trust; time; the capacity to tolerate ambiguity and anxiety, to resist quick fixes and premature judgments, to struggle for authentic understanding, and to appreciate detail, nuance, and tacit knowledge; and the involvement of external partners.

We learn about diverse kinds of and approaches to inquiry with diverse stakeholders in four diverse contexts over a 3–4-year period. Descriptions of the practicalities provide practitioners and reformers with a guide for pursuing collaborative inquiry, including the entry points and the milestones as well as how teachers identify important questions, use classroom data for inquiry, develop facilitation and technical skills and norms of behavior, and find time to meet. In this volume readers will find resources, examples of practice, dilemmas, and questions.

But perhaps most significantly, the authors explore difficult issues such as the movement from inquiry to conversations to insights to action that "will make a difference in student learning." And they show faculty struggling with these issues along with images of changes in teachers' practice. These explorations of collaborative inquiry remind us of how school communities benefit from the construction and dissemination of new knowledge that emanates from a close examination of teachers' own work and that of their colleagues and their students, the renewal of the school as a learning community, and the adoption of a whole-school inquiry stance to ensure that all students derive the benefits of reflective practice.

At the heart of this book is a profound belief in the possibilities of teaching and of the student-teacher-"text" relationship. It offers a refreshing optimism along with the powerful reminder that the possibilities for student learning will mirror the possibilities for teacher learning, and it builds a strong case for the importance of nurturing a culture of professional learning in schools. Gently but in a steadfastly compelling way, the authors capture the dignity of teaching at a time when that dignity needs rescuing.

Ann Lieberman and
Jacqueline Ancess

Acknowledgments

The authors wish to thank the Wallace Foundation for generously supporting the three projects described in this book. We especially want to thank Carla Ascher, program officer; Edward Pauly, director of evaluation; and Mary Lee Fitzgerald, director of education programs, who provided intellectual and moral support for our projects.

We are also grateful for the Wallace Foundation's support of the National Study Group, a cohort that met twice a year to reflect on our experiences. This group included members of the three projects—both participating school and project staff. Also at the table were national experts in professional development and inquiry approaches to school improvement: Ann Lieberman of the Carnegie Foundation for the Advancement of Teaching; Jacqueline Ancess of the National Center for Restructuring Education, Schools and Teaching at Teachers College; and Lew Allen of the League of Professional Schools. An evaluation team from the University of California, Berkeley, led by Judith Warren Little with Maryl Gearhart, Judith Kafka, and Marnie Curry, also joined the group. All of these participants were critical friends in the best sense of the word and provided varied and useful perspectives on our work.

The authors wish to thank the following schools, districts, organizations, and individuals whose work is highlighted in the case studies in Part II of the book.

ASCEND Middle School (Oakland, California Public Schools): We would like to thank Elena Aguilar, a teacher with an inspirational love of students, teaching, and researching; Hae-Sin Kim for her strong leadership, which has made ASCEND an exceptional school for students and staff; and the excellent and devoted ASCEND staff, especially inquiry colleagues Davina Katz and Stephanie Sisk-Hilton.

Maxson Middle School (Plainfield, New Jersey Public Schools): We would like to thank the following people from the Plainfield, New Jersey school district and Maxson Middle School. They include staff developers Sandy Bidwell and Patricia van Langen, whose leadership and commitment to the improvement of teaching were critical to implementing this initiative; Linnea Weiland, the director of curriculum and instruction, who was a consistent champion of this work; Mark Jackson, the principal, who participated in many sessions on reviewing student work to learn its challenges and benefits so that he could better support it in his school; and the teachers from the MIT school of choice—Jerome Jackson, Miriam Malabanan, Stephanie Dubrow, Carrie Hittel, and Kurt Faunce.

Harbor Middle School (Boston, Massachusetts Public Schools): The effort of several people at the Harbor School were instrumental in launching the work and supporting it through its development. They include Scott Hartl, the school director; Joe Zaremba, teacher facilitator and project coordinator for the school; Christina Patterson, teacher curriculum coordinator and facilitator; Mark Clarke, teacher and facilitator; Karen Engel, teacher and facilitator; Suzanne Plaut, administrative intern and special projects coordinator; and Barbara van Allen Browne, special education coordinator and facilitator.

Melrose Elementary School (Oakland, California Public Schools): We would like to thank the teachers on Melrose's Sheltered English Team (2000–02) for their cooperation, their collegiality, their feedback, and most of all for their inspiring work: Matt Behnke, Dorothy Cotton, Marla Kamiya, Sue Jones, Tarie Lewis, Terry Tasby, and Katie Thompson. We also want to extend our appreciation to the Melrose principal, Moyra Contreras, for her leadership over the years, and to Melrose teacher Sarah Capitelli for her insight and feedback.

The case studies of ASCEND and Melrose were written by Elizabeth Simons and Tom Malarkey, colleagues from the CES regional center based in Oakland, California, the Bay Area Coalition of Equitable Schools (BayCES). We are extremely grateful for their significant contribution to this volume. Liz and Tom wish to acknowledge the support of their colleagues at BayCES, in particular, Tony Smith, Zaretta Hammond, and Margaret Perrow.

We also wish to thank the Walter and Elise Haas Fund for supporting the Teacher Inquiry Project, of which these schools are a part.

In addition to the case study schools, we would like to thank the staff and administrators from the following schools, districts, and organizations, which collaborated with us on the projects described in the book: Alameda County Office of Education, Oakland, CA; Beeber Middle School, Philadelphia; Coalition of Essential Schools Northwest; Expeditionary Learning/Outward Bound; Fisher Hill Elementary School, Orange, MA; Hubbard Middle School, Plainfield, NJ; Jacob Hiatt Magnet School, Worcester, MA; Lamberton Middle School, Philadelphia; Museum of Children's Art, Oakland, CA; Overbrook Education Center, Philadelphia; Renaissance Program at the Forestdale School, Malden, MA; Southern Maine Partnership.

Finally the authors would like to thank the following individuals who contributed to our projects and the development of this book: Carlos

Alberto, Kelly Allyn, Rolynn Anderson, Barbara Andrews, Margarita Baez, Mackensey Bailey, Debra Beauregard, Cynthia Blumsack, Celia Bouffidis, Sheryl Brault, Tom Brindisi, David Brown, Connie Bunker, Tony Caputo, Ann Caren, Lisa Casaletto, Dorie Cerruti, Maurine Chirichetti, Linda Clark, Kathleen Colligan, Beth Corrigan, Winston Cox, Margery Deane, Martha Dewar, Sylvia Di Lorenzo, Sheila Drapiewski, Beth Dunn, Deanna Federman, Sherry Flynn, Linda Friedrich, Ted Friend, Sandy Gabrielian, Amy Gerstein, Terry Grey, Bill Hanscom, Sandra Harrison, Carol Hawley, Sara Hendren, Joel Jaroch, Chante Jillson, Deborah Jumpp, Susan Hunt Apteker, Marlys Kirschner, Sheryl Klein, Mary Labuski, Gwen Larsen, Patricia Leon, Larry Leverett, Nicole Liss, Olivia Lynch, John Maccario, Elaine McCarthy, Lois McGee, Kate McGovern, Shirley McPhillips, Cheryl Metevier, Patrick Montesano, Kathy Moragne, Louise Music, Kari Nelsestuen, John Newlin, Moira O'Brien, Patty Padilla, Thomas Patterson, Jala Olds-Pearson, Gail Peddle, Linda Ponce de Leon, Warren Pross, Sue Proulx, Miriam Raider-Roth, Janet Reeder, Jane Remer, David Ruff, Lydia Scarbriel, Arlene Schmaeff, Mary Rita Sheldon, Amanda Siano, Ruby Simmons, Denise Simon, Armita Sims, Tonia Slay-Daniels, Steven Surette, Terry Tasby, Kelly Therrien, Janice Thomas, Valerie Thompson, Irene Tsoules, Terri Turner, Helena Valentine, Shirley Veenema, Ruth Verock-O'Loughlin, Renee Wearing, David Weinstein, Elaine Wetterauer, Brian White, Barbara Winokur, Frank Wirmusky.

Special thanks also go to Elayne Archer (AED) and Cecelia Cancellaro for their thoughtful editing, and to Frances Segura (AED) for her patience and skill in compiling the manuscript.

The five coauthors would also like to acknowledge Alexandra Weinbaum (AED), whose vision, determination, and skill supported our collaborative inquiry and ultimately made this book possible.

Turning Classroom Experience into Teaching Expertise

Consider a familiar story with a not-so-familiar ending. Its beginning is like many stories of teachers' work in many districts: A district, at the request of the state department of education, adopts a new language skills curriculum and requires that every teacher in the district implement it. In the typical story, teachers would have responded with feelings of frustration and anger: Why are we being forced to teach in a certain way? The mandated approach doesn't meet the needs of our students as we see them. Why doesn't the district value the experience and expertise that we have? Confused by the plethora of such mandates and disheartened by the sense of being prevented from exercising their professional skills and judgment, the teachers would have begun to feel more like "paper pushers" than productive and trusted professionals.

So might the usual events unfold around a new district mandate. But this story departs from that script. Within months of the new mandate, a group of teachers in the district is engaged in rigorous discussion of the new curriculum. Some members of the group are piloting parts of it, and the teachers meet on a regular basis to evaluate the lessons that have been taught, consider their effectiveness, compare them to similar lessons they've tried in the past, and develop ways of enhancing and supplementing the new material. For these teachers, the mandate has evolved into an opportunity to reconsider and discuss long-held beliefs about how language skills are taught in their classrooms.

What makes the difference? Why, when so many teachers respond to such district and state mandates with a growing sense of helplessness and hopelessness, were these teachers able to engage the new curriculum productively, thoughtfully, and professionally?

In this particular school, two key features made the difference: a principal who saw and supported collaborative inquiry as a way for teachers to engage deeply with their own questions, and a history of collaborative inquiry that enabled the teachers in this group to undertake and carry out their own inquiry process. Initially, some of these teachers had greeted the mandate with all the skeptical responses that teachers often do: Why does anyone think this is better than what I'm already doing? When am I going to have the time to develop a whole new set of lessons? Maybe I can just lay low, and This, too, shall pass. However, their school's long-standing commitment to a culture of collaborative inquiry gave these teachers both the opportunity and the support to turn their questions into a serious quest. Through inquiry, the teachers sought a deeper understanding of complex issues, including how students learn language skills, how teachers can best assist them in that learning, and how the mandated curriculum might fit into that effort.

COLLABORATIVE INQUIRY IN PRACTICE

Collaborative inquiry, however, isn't just a way to respond productively to district or state mandates. Consider these other situations in which collaborative inquiry plays a key role:

- A school faculty wants to learn where its students are struggling the most in the development of critical thinking skills in math and science. A collaborative inquiry group is formed to allow math and science teachers to pursue this question through regular examination and analysis of student work.
- Some teachers in a school want to help their students become more reflective learners, able to self-assess and self-edit their work. They form a collaborative inquiry group to explore what it means to be a "reflective learner" and how students can best develop that capacity.
- A school wants to look closely at issues of equity in its own community: Why do some groups of students fare better on standardized tests and/or classroom assessments than students from other groups? What can be done to close the gap? Collaborative inquiry groups form to study various kinds of data that reveal the nature of the gap and to develop strategies for tackling the problem.

DEFINING COLLABORATIVE INQUIRY

What is collaborative inquiry? In its simplest terms, collaborative inquiry is the process by which colleagues gather in groups to pursue, over time, the questions about teaching and learning that the group members identify as important. Groups develop their understanding of an issue through framing a question, identifying artifacts or "evidence" that help respond to it, sharing perspectives on the evidence, reflecting on the partial or provisional answers that emerge, and revising the question in light of experiences and discussion. Through collaborative inquiry, teachers make sense of their experiences in the classroom, learn from those experiences, and draw upon the perspectives of colleagues to enhance their teaching and their students' learning (Bray, Lee, Smith, & Yorks, 2000; Carini, 2001; Clark, 2001; Cochran-Smith & Lytle, 1999).

The steps of the inquiry process might be presented as a straight line that progresses from identifying questions through gathering and analyzing data to generating new teaching approaches that address the questions and generate others. (See Chapter 3 for a sample inquiry process.) In practice, as you will see, the process is much less orderly, sometimes lingering on one part for weeks, sometimes moving back and forth between two parts before moving on to a third. Each part of the collaborative inquiry process involves its own subprocesses and responds to subtle and not-so-subtle differences in the context in which it is carried out. For example, "identifying questions" is itself a complex set of tasks and experiences rich with the potential for learning.

Collaborative inquiry does not always lead to direct or easily applicable solutions. But when carried out over time, thoughtfully, and with support and resources, it leads to deeper understanding of the question, which too often is the missing precondition for seeing new possibilities and, ultimately, for making change.

WHY WE VALUE COLLABORATIVE INQUIRY

The authors of this book and the organizations we represent come to this work with convictions and values that have both grown out of, and informed, our work with students, teachers, schools, and districts. These convictions are rooted in decades of research carried out by our organizations, as well as by others, on how children and adults learn, how organizations change, and how educators develop as professionals. Chapter 1 provides a more detailed summary of the research that has the most direct implications for our work. Here, we highlight the foundational beliefs that underpin our commitment to collaborative inquiry as a powerful, though complex and demanding, form of professional development in schools:

Beliefs About Teaching and Learning

Teaching and learning, rather than being dichotomous, are in fact inextricably linked and, indeed, share many of the same features. Good teaching is often a matter of educators' willingness and ability to learn from students: to see in the way that students see and to appreciate how students make sense of their world. We believe that both teaching and learning need to be made visible and public—examined and discussed by groups of educators and interested others—in order for both to be improved. One of the most important (and most overlooked) sources of data about classroom teaching and learning is the work that both students and teachers do on a daily basis. While scores on standardized tests may capture some aspects of student learning, they can never reveal learning in all its complexity, nor offer enough detail and context to help teachers improve their practice. We also believe that learning and teaching are fundamentally social and emotional activities as well as cognitive activities. Therefore, any approach attempting to improve learning and teaching must address the social and emotional as well as cognitive needs of teachers and students.

Beliefs About Teachers

Teachers are professionals who have developed expertise born of their experience in the classroom and their preservice and in-service professional development opportunities. We believe that teachers, like all professionals, can further develop their expertise through focused discussion and analysis with colleagues and interested outsiders as they reflect on and improve their practice. When provided with time and support, teachers can identify the key problems and issues that need to be addressed in order to help improve teaching and learning in their classrooms and schools.

Beliefs About the Context of Schools

Each school context is unique. Different student bodies come with different strengths and needs. Different faculties represent varied experiences, disparate beliefs about learning, and diverse interests and skills. The communities from which the students come have concerns, strengths, and resources that vary across districts, let alone states and the country as a whole. The history of the connection between the school and the parent community differs from school to school. In the face of such diversity, teachers need to consider how broader issues of policy (curriculum framework, standards, and so on) can be addressed in their own unique contexts. While schools and teachers can benefit from the thoughtful work that is carried out in other places, they need to consider carefully how that work can be applied to the questions and concerns that are most relevant for them, their students, and their broader school community. Educators do not have to reinvent the wheel, but they do need to adapt the wheel in ways appropriate for their own students and the communities from which those students come. The ability to apply any mandate locally is greatly informed and enhanced by inquiry.

WHAT MAKES COLLABORATIVE INQUIRY UNIQUE?

Of course, collaborative inquiry is not the only process for supporting improved learning and teaching in schools. Other opportunities, including workshops, seminars, courses, conferences, and coaching or mentoring systems, play important roles as well. However, collaborative inquiry, anchored in the values described above, supports several critical needs of teachers as professionals—needs not typically met in any other way. Collaborative inquiry offers teachers an opportunity to create professional development opportunities with their colleagues that are relevant to their classrooms and help them develop as professionals. It offers a professional development structure that can change over time in response to teachers' changing needs and growth. When teachers and administrators work together in groups, sharing their results, collaborative inquiry can feed whole-school reform. Collaborative inquiry gives teachers a chance to engage in the kind of learning they promote with their own students. Some of the unique features of collaborative inquiry are captured below in the words of teachers who have been involved in collaborative inquiry groups:

- *Collaborative inquiry enables colleagues to explore issues that they themselves identify as important.* "This is the only place I can come where someone else isn't telling me what I should be paying attention to, what I need to be doing. We decide what we need to talk about, given what's going on in our teaching lives."
- *Collaborative inquiry enables teachers to overcome concerns about making their work public.* "I realized in that conversation that my colleagues were really there to help me . . . that we were all thinking about how we could all improve our teaching and the kids' learning. They weren't there to tell me that I had done this or that wrong."
- *Collaborative inquiry provides teachers with the opportunity to obtain fresh perspectives on their students, their students' work, and their own work.* "Sometimes I look at things and I don't see them. I become so involved that I'm losing sight of what is really there, and what is not there. I can't distance myself and sometimes I don't know where to

go next. Sometimes, I just need someone to know about this, so that someone else sees it, and this gets me moving again."

- *Collaborative inquiry renews teachers, providing them with opportunities for intellectual growth and engagement that sustain them through the often-draining work of teaching.* "I feel like my spirit and my teaching have been rejuvenated . . . The changes I'm making are giving me the energy to keep going. I'm looking at my teaching with different eyes. The ability to change is keeping me interested."

WHAT MAKES COLLABORATIVE INQUIRY POSSIBLE?

The work of a collaborative inquiry group is challenging. Identifying important questions and figuring out ways to pursue them is time-consuming and often painstaking work. In addition, creating the structures and finding the resources to properly support collaborative inquiry is difficult. Finding time in the school schedule for regular meetings is a perpetual challenge, with financial as well as logistical implications. Simply maintaining ongoing communication among members of a collaborative inquiry group in a school setting can be tricky. Furthermore, actually doing something with what one has learned through inquiry—experimenting with new teaching ideas in the classroom, throwing out practices one had relied upon, and so on—can be difficult. But these problems are solvable if school and district leaders have the will to support collaborative inquiry and if the potential participants find the articulated purposes of the collaborative inquiry—and the work itself—compelling.

As will be shown in the following pages, working on the collaborative inquiry projects described in this book tested the will and commitment of teachers, administrators, and researchers alike and, in doing so, surfaced many lessons, including some skills and strategies that make collaborative inquiry both possible and powerful. These include:

- Learning to identify important questions.
- Selecting and using data from the classroom—student work, assignments, units, and so on—for inquiry.
- Developing technical skills of facilitation and using structures for conversations.
- Making time in the school day to engage in inquiry.

Chapter 2 provides a more detailed analysis of these, as well as other, key strategies used in schools undertaking collaborative inquiry work.

THE ORGANIZATIONS AND RESEARCH BEHIND THIS BOOK

To understand more about the challenges of collaborative inquiry, the three "author organizations" of this book—the Academy for Educational Development, the Coalition of Essential Schools, and Project Zero at the Harvard Graduate School of Education—each embarked on its own project in partnership with various schools and/or districts to establish, support, and document collaborative inquiry groups in schools.

The Academy for Educational Development (AED) is an independent, nonprofit organization committed to addressing human development and educational needs in the United States and throughout the world. AED's Center for School and Community Services uses multidisciplinary approaches to address key issues in education, health, and youth development. AED's work is informed by the core values of equity, excellence, collaboration, and democratic participation. The AED project entitled Reviewing Student Work/Improving Student Achievement sought to build the capacity of school faculties in five schools across two districts in order to improve the quality of instruction in the middle grades through a continuous, comprehensive, whole-school and team review of student work.

The Coalition of Essential Schools (CES) is an independent, nonprofit organization that supports schools that seek to enact the CES Common Principles. The Common Principles promote school designs, curricula, and pedagogies that support active, engaged learning; small, caring communities; and democratic, equitable school practices. The experiences of two CES projects are represented in this book: Improving Instruction through Inquiry and Collaboration sought to support the faculties at six middle and high schools in Washington State and Maine to develop collaborative inquiry groups for the purpose of improving the quality of instruction; and the Teacher Inquiry Project, implemented by the Bay Area Coalition for Equitable Schools (BayCES—the CES regional center located in Oakland, California) focused particularly on equity, highlighting the potential power of inquiry projects to help teachers serve low-achieving students more effectively.

Project Zero, based at the Harvard Graduate School of Education, is a research group dedicated to understanding and enhancing learning, thinking, and creativity for individuals and groups in schools as well as in other institutions (community arts centers, museums, corporations, and other kinds of organizations). A central element of Project Zero's work over the past 15 years has been developing and researching processes for enabling groups of teachers to assess student work collaboratively. The Evidence Project, a collaboration with four Massachusetts elementary and middle schools, focused on embedding teachers' collaborative assessment of student work in an ongoing cycle of inquiry in order to enable teachers to improve classroom instruction.

The schools with which each organization worked spanned a variety of settings and situations. They included rural, small town, suburban, and urban schools. The largest school had a student body of about 1,000 while the smallest served 180 students. Most of the schools predominantly served populations of students from low-income families, and a number of them served primarily African American, Latino, and Asian students.

THE DEVELOPMENT OF THIS BOOK

In many ways, this book is the result of our own collaborative inquiry, both within and across the three organizations. Much of the cross-organization collaborative work happened through regular meetings convened by the Wallace Foundation. These meetings brought together staff from the three organizations, teachers and administrators from the schools and districts each organization partnered with, and an extraordinary group of scholars and researchers from the University of California, Berkeley; the League of Professional Schools; the National Center for Restructuring Education, Schools, and Teaching; and the Carnegie Center for the Advancement of Teaching.

In these cross-group meetings, we practiced many of the forms of inquiry described in these pages. Our experience also mirrored that of collaborative inquiry groups in schools, including the early anxieties about sharing our work with one another, even though we were working in a supportive group of like-minded colleagues. And, as many collaborative inquiry groups do, we experienced the gradual deepening of learning that comes from inquiry. That it took us 4 years to reach the point of sharing some of the results of that work in this format is a mark not just of the challenges of writing a book about a complex subject, but also an important reminder that, regardless of setting, collaborative inquiry needs time to develop if it is to be fruitful (and multiply!).

Voice, Audience, and Structure

Throughout the development of this book, the six authors have worked to compare, contrast, analyze, and synthesize our organizations' various experiences. With the exception of the case studies, all parts of this book have been written with a single authorial voice that represents all six of us. In order to preserve the particular nuances of the individual case studies (which represent the various projects we have brought together), each of those was written only by people who were directly involved with the schools and districts depicted. The case study authors include three who are not named on the volume as a whole: Tom Malarkey and Elizabeth Simons of the Bay Area Coalition for Equitable Schools, and Kari Nelsestuen of the Academy for Educational Development.

Like collaborative inquiry itself, this book stands at the meeting place of theory and practice. In it, we share some of the experiences, frameworks, and analyses that grew out of our 3 years of work in facilitating and researching collaborative inquiry groups in schools. Although it is not specifically a handbook on how to do collaborative inquiry, much of it will be helpful to those who are engaged in that activity or who would like to be. In addition, much of it will be useful to researchers who are interested in delving more deeply into purposes, processes, and products of collaborative inquiry.

The Organization of This Book

The book is divided into three main parts. Part I, comprising Chapters 1 and 2, offers an initial grounding in the theory and practice of collaborative inquiry. Chapter 1 presents a range of research that establishes the basis for collaborative inquiry, while Chapter 2, growing out of our own research, details key decision points that groups and schools need to make in establishing and sustaining collaborative inquiry as a process, including framing the purposes for inquiry.

Part II focuses on the particular work carried out by our organizations and our partner schools. At its heart are four chapter-long case studies. The cases offer stories and voices from the sites and from teachers with whom we worked. Taken as a group, they allow glimpses into collaborative inquiry as it operates in different contexts and with different constituents: a single teacher whose individual inquiry work sparks school-wide work; a single group within a school in a district that has mandated inquiry groups; a new school just beginning collaborative inquiry; and an established school with a history of inquiry. Interspersed with the case studies are several sections that introduce them as a group and provide brief analyses of individual case studies.

Part III comprises Chapters 7 and 8, which discuss milestones in inquiry and the policy and research questions that are central to future explorations of collaborative inquiry as an important form of school improvement.

Collaborative inquiry is a complex process—one that raises many questions: How does collaborative inquiry help educators uncover and make sense of the complexity of their own and their students' daily experiences in schools and classrooms? What kinds of time and tools do educators need in order to carry out inquiry well? How can collaborative inquiry nurture teachers' inclination to question their own practices? And what is needed to help inquiry evolve into the regular practice that educators pursue with the persistence and rigor that will lead to a quality education for *all* students?

We hope this book helps you both to think more deeply about these questions and to pose your own. It offers resources, possibilities, illustrations—and more questions. Indeed, this book represents our own continuing quest for a more complete understanding of the collaborative inquiry process. We invite you to join us.

Part I

Making the Case

The two chapters in this part provide the theoretical framework for the rest of the book. Chapter 1 provides an overview of research on collaborative inquiry in schools. Its six sections—Learning and Inquiry, Teacher Professional Development and Collaborative Inquiry, Reflection and Inquiry, The Emotional Dimension of Inquiry, Organizational Learning and Inquiry, and The Culture and Values of Inquiring Schools—underscore both the complexity of the topic and the centrality of collaborative inquiry to effective teaching and student learning, as well as to organizational learning. In its conclusion, the chapter presents a framework for thinking about the characteristics of schools in which "inquiry" becomes a habit—schools in which teachers continuously engage with peers in questioning their own practice and finding solutions to those questions that support student learning. The chapter emphasizes key points that are illustrated and enlarged upon in Parts II and III: Collaborative inquiry is intellectually challenging, emotionally demanding, and as much art as science; its outcomes depend as much on the courage to ask difficult and vexing questions as on the skills and knowledge needed to create powerful learning communities among teachers.

Chapter 2 provides an overview of how schools go about the business of setting up effective collaborative inquiry groups. It does this through examining how schools and people within them define—and continually refine—the purposes for inquiry, which vary enormously from school to school and even among groups of teachers within schools. It moves to consider the key decisions about how to pursue inquiry. The chapter asks teachers and administrators to consider a number of critical issues in developing inquiry in schools. These questions are: What are the central questions that guide the inquiry conversation and the data that will be used to address them? Which teachers will take part and in what combination? How will teachers address the central questions that they posed, and which protocols, norms, and other tools are needed to support effective inquiry? How will the inquiry process be supported through incentives, allocation of time for the work, involvement of external partners, and so forth? The chapter also discusses the importance of ensuring that the relationships between the purposes and the processes of inquiry are clearly thought through and continuously revisited. The decisions reached about purposes and processes involve every aspect of schooling—organization and resources, philosophy and pedagogy, individual and group differences among staff and students, external partners, and group facilitation issues. The chapter provides many examples from the literature, the cases in this book, and other documented inquiry experiences to provide a context for understanding the relationship of purposes and processes to creating a productive inquiry.

Chapter 1

Foundations for Inquiry: Reviewing the Research

The purpose of this chapter is twofold: to present research supporting the centrality of inquiry to effective teaching and student learning, as well as to organizational learning; and to discuss the values and culture of schools in which collaborative and sustained teacher inquiry is a habit. Connecting each of the six major sections is the idea that collaborative inquiry is central to how all people learn—how children and adults learn, how teachers learn through professional development, and how organizations, including schools, learn.

INTRODUCTION

Collaborative, sustained inquiry into teaching and learning is the exception rather than the rule in most U.S. schools. Its absence (beyond the review of test data) is striking, particularly when compared with several European countries as well as Japan, where it is routinely practiced and integrated into the school day. Even before the pressures of the current accountability policy, few schools or districts created time during the day or devoted resources to making teacher inquiry a reality.

Barriers to Inquiry

The absence of time within the school day is often cited as the major barrier to regular collaborative teacher inquiry. An alternative explanation is that time is not set aside for inquiry because inquiry has not been valued as a means to improve schools or teaching. The current policy context is averse to inquiry in many ways. High-stakes testing has narrowed curriculum and instruction to focus on test preparation, and the demands of the external accountability system have focused teacher inquiry, to the extent it is practiced, on analyzing test data so that teachers can better prepare students for the tests.

While the narrowing of the curriculum to address current accountability policies is a relatively recent aspect of the education policy landscape, our school systems' focus on bureaucratic control and accountability has a long history, leaving the most important aspect of school—the quality of teaching—largely to the discretion of individual teachers.

In contrast to schools in which teachers view themselves as solo performers, schools that develop an "inquiry stance," a term coined by researchers Marilyn Cochran-Smith and Susan Lytle (1999), create constructive opportunities for teachers to question their practices in the light of external research, the unique needs of their student body, and the history and context of their school and its surrounding community.

Lack of Research on Inquiry

Because collaborative, sustained inquiry over time is atypical in our schools, there is not yet a body of research that can provide adequate evidence for the effectiveness of all the approaches to inquiry on student learning and teacher development. However, recent research on professional development that includes ongoing inquiry into practice—for example, through such professional networks as the National Writing Project and "critical friends groups"—demonstrates that teachers' development is profoundly and positively affected by their participation in inquiry. Their professional competence and confidence are reflected in the quality of their instructional practices and in the quality of student work from their classrooms (Academy for Educational Development [AED], 2002a; Clark, 2001; Lieberman & Wood, 2003; Richardson, 2003).

In their review of quasi-experimental studies of teachers reviewing student work, Judith Warren Little and her colleagues (2003) found a positive impact of this type of inquiry on student academic outcomes and on observed and self-reported teacher practice and knowledge. However, they also point out that the "black box" of teacher inquiry into student work and instruction has not yet been sufficiently explored. Researchers have limited knowledge about what happens in the various kinds of inquiry groups or how particular practices relate to student outcomes and teacher development. The cases in Chapters 3 through 6 in this book provide concrete images of what such practice looks like in real schools and how it is related to improvements in instruction and student outcomes.

This chapter contains six sections:

Learning and Inquiry discusses the scientific research substantiating the importance of inquiry approaches for students and adults to learn concepts rather than facts.

Teacher Professional Development and Collaborative Inquiry discusses recent research on professional development, which, like research on how people learn, demonstrates that effective learning for teachers must include inquiry into their own classrooms.

Reflection and Inquiry discusses the importance of reflection in inquiry and why it is essential for effective inquiry work among teachers.

The Emotional Dimension of Inquiry discusses research that demonstrates that, because learning requires the recognition and understanding of preconceptions and sometimes substantial rethinking of previously held ideas, it has a strong affective dimension.

Organizational Learning and Inquiry summarizes research on how organizations, as opposed to individuals, learn, and the role of inquiry in organizational learning.

The Culture and Values of Inquiring Schools summarizes the lessons from a 5-year study of a California elementary school as well as research on "trusting relationships" in schools, to describe the conditions that make teacher inquiry possible and effective.

LEARNING AND INQUIRY

Based on research in many domains of science about brain functioning and how children learn in various settings, a recent National Research Council (NRC) study, *How People Learn: Brain, Mind, Experience and School* (2000) highlights three key activities that must occur to ensure a deep understanding of subject matter. These activities include identifying preconceptions, relating new factual information to a conceptual framework(s), and monitoring and assessing learning.

Identifying or "Surfacing" Preconceptions

To learn effectively and help others learn, we must identify our preconceptions about the world and human relations. These preconceptions help us make "order out of the chaos" of the ideas, impressions, information, and sensations that we receive every moment of the day. A Harvard–Smithsonian study (Shapiro, 1987) in which high school students and graduate students from Harvard were asked the reasons for the change in seasons revealed that virtually all of them assumed that the seasons are caused by the earth's distance from the sun rather than by the tilt of the earth in relation to the sun. Graduate students offered responses no different from that of ninth graders in public schools. Even when students had been taught the correct reasons for the changing seasons, their preconceptions were what remained after the lessons had been forgotten. Such preconceptions will "trump" new learning if students do not have opportunities to examine them and learn factual material through a new framework.

Relating New Factual Information to a Conceptual Framework(s)

The process of learning is one of constructing meaning from new information by using conceptual frameworks. An understanding of factual information within a conceptual framework allows students to organize new information and retrieve and retain it. When factual information is learned without a conceptual framework—as a list of facts to be memorized—it is usually forgotten in short order.

Monitoring and Assessing Learning

Students need to develop a process to monitor and assess their learning and performance. Experts in all fields, in contrast to novices, are able to reflect on their performance and self-correct. Similarly, students need to take control of their learning by developing the capacity to self-assess: Am I understanding, and how well? What else do I need to know and do to develop my understanding? How can I demonstrate my understanding?

Research on adult learning emphasizes a similar process in conceptual learning. In *Learning as Transformation* (Mezirow & Associates, 2001), the contributing authors distinguish between two types of learning—informative and transformative. Informative learning entails the acquisition of what might be regarded as factual knowledge, while transformative learning involves the process by which we revise or change our fundamental assumptions, perspectives, and worldviews (Mezirow & Associates, 2001). Most adults, including teachers, have been schooled in the practice of absorbing new information quickly and reproducing it on tests. Indeed, most of us had a 16-year apprenticeship in "teaching as telling and learning as memorizing" (Ball & Cohen, 1999). It is partly because of this early immersion in acquiring factual knowledge that teaching approaches, for the most part, have remained remarkably resilient to change, focusing, to a great degree, on the student acquisition of knowledge.

Most traditional forms of professional development focus on the acquisition of new information—new content in a subject area or new teaching strategies. This kind of learning is important, but teachers also need a deep understanding of their subject matter, grounded in multiple examples and applications and appropriate pedagogy as well as a deep understanding about how their students learn. They must monitor their own learning in a way that allows for openness, questioning, and adjustments. This kind of transformative learning rarely occurs in traditional forms of professional development, such as the "one-shot" in-service workshop, and is more likely to occur in sustained collaborative inquiry, which is described below.

TEACHER PROFESSIONAL DEVELOPMENT AND COLLABORATIVE INQUIRY

There is virtual agreement among researchers that new ways of teaching and the need to foster learning communities among teachers require new forms of professional development. Researchers of every stripe agree that professional development should be long-term and frequent, have a strong school-based component, enable teachers to consider their teaching in light of research and their own practice, be grounded in teaching and student learning, and be linked to curricula (McLaughlin & Talbert, 2001). In addition, professional development must tap teachers' knowledge, build on their questions, and help and support them in evaluating their beliefs, and sometimes in changing deeply embedded behaviors. In their discussion of professional development, Deborah Ball and David Cohen (1999) argue that it must be grounded in teaching as it is carried out daily; not to do this is like asking someone "to learn to swim on a sidewalk" (p. 12). The National Research Council report (2000) stresses that learning in teacher preparation courses, as well as in professional development, must parallel that of their students.

The Value of Inquiry Groups

Collaborative inquiry groups are a vehicle for fostering these new requirements of professional development. These groups are based on the notion, common to other professions such as medicine or law, that experts and novices learn from cases presented by their peers. When teachers present a lesson, samples of several students' work, or the work of a struggling student to their peers, they are, in effect, presenting "cases." The ensuing discussion draws on their collective experiences; it may also draw on district and state standards, curriculum, and possibly on new research. Inquiry groups provide a place for both experienced professionals and those in the earlier stages of their career to hone their craft and support one another. The more experienced staff bring insights from their many years of work, but they may also resist change more than newer staff, who must change continuously as they learn their craft.

Some researchers (Cochran-Smith & Lytle, 1999; Hiebert, Gallimore, & Stigler, 2002) argue that the knowledge produced by teachers in inquiry groups is unique and potentially uniquely beneficial to the improvement of practice. They argue that research about instruction is not used often by teachers because it isolates variables in instruction from their contexts. An understanding of these contexts and of particular students is precisely what concerns teachers in their daily practice. In collaborative inquiry groups, teachers construct knowledge from questioning their own practice and looking closely at their own students and their work.

Developing an "Inquiry Stance"

Cochran-Smith and Lytle (1999) argue that to use inquiry effectively, teachers must develop an "inquiry stance," which tolerates uncertainty and shuns the "quick fix." Such a stance opens everything to questioning, including research from university-based researchers, suggestions from expert teachers, and accepted ways of teaching that may appear to "work." Hiebert, Gallimore, and Stigler (2002) believe that teacher inquiry, when properly conducted and represented, may yield the most useful research for the field. Indeed, these authors describe a knowledge base constructed over time by teachers as they assess their work and that of their students, represent it to their colleagues, and make the information public and retrievable electronically.

These researchers emphasize that to make the knowledge that teachers produce usable by others, teachers must learn to represent their work publicly, select artifacts from their teaching and student work and store them electronically, and make them accessible through various formats—both virtual and real, with commentary/discussion by teachers and outside researchers. Through these formats, teachers can contribute to a teacher-researcher-based discourse about teaching and learning. While such an image of knowledge production and sharing is a thing of the future, it does point to the potential centrality of teacher inquiry groups in producing useful knowledge for the classroom.

REFLECTION AND INQUIRY

A further characteristic of inquiry groups is that, unlike the quick-fix in-service workshop, they provide time for ongoing reflection, an extraordinarily scarce commodity for most teachers. Although an important part of the inquiry process, reflection is not always built into it. Reflection demands that teachers avoid making immediate judgments about data under consideration, whether it be a piece of student work, an assignment, or a video of an instructional unit, and take the time to see and describe "what is there."

Although teachers may reflect on their own practice in the classroom, and perhaps privately afterward, they seldom have the opportunity to do this with their peers. In her study of the role of reflection in professional development, Carol Rodgers (2002) makes the analogy between a teacher's ability to "see" his or her students' learning and that of an artist. An artist's sensibility demands "a high level of consciousness about what one sees . . . a fine attention to detail and form; the perception of relations (tensions and harmonies); the perception of nuance (colors and meaning); [and] the perception of changes (shifts and subtle motions)" (McCrary, 2000, pp. 221–222). Educators require a similar sensibility, which can only be developed through reflection, detached from the daily demands of school and in collaboration with one's peers.

Rodgers's approach to collaborative reflection is based on the work of John Dewey and that of the Prospect Center in Vermont, founded by Patricia Carini. Carini calls on teachers to learn to become more mindful of their practice through careful description of what takes place in the classroom or in a piece of student work. She argues that too often we jump to conclusions without the benefit of truly examining "what is there" or having the benefit of others' perspectives. In her cycle of reflection, the act of "attending to and describing" demands that teachers withhold judgment or interpretation. A teacher might present something troubling from her or his classroom, a video of a lesson, or a sample of student work. It is important that participating teachers describe what they see, while withholding judgment. This allows teachers to "re-see" their classroom or a piece of student work in a new light. Such "re-seeing" permits teachers to unravel and "surface" their preconceptions and recognize alternative interpretations of teaching and student work or behavior (Carini, 2001).

The parallel between an artist's and a teacher's way of seeing is captured in the following description by a teacher of his collaborative inquiry group as a "poetry meeting":

> In our lives we were all like firemen. We were putting out fires and then suddenly we went to this poetry meeting . . . If you are fighting fires, poetry becomes insignificant. But if your entire life is spent without poetry in it, then what is the meaning of your life? (Kasl & Yorks, 2002, p. 15)

In short, at its best, professional development incorporating sustained inquiry into and reflection on teacher practice combines the mindfulness of artists with the inquiring and open-mindedness of researchers. It provides the time for standing back and reflecting, and reminds people why they became teachers in the first place. It returns them to the core of the profession—a commitment to student learning.

THE EMOTIONAL DIMENSION OF INQUIRY

Because learning requires the recognition and understanding of preconceptions and sometimes substantial rethinking of previously held ideas, it
has a strong affective dimension. The vignette below suggests the power of
an inquiry group for unraveling assumptions about teaching, as well as the
"affective" challenges to making changes in the classroom.

> A second-year seventh-grade science teacher participated in an
> ongoing inquiry group with four other teachers from her interdisci-
> plinary grade-level team. Periodically they met to discuss their
> students' work, focusing on a mutually agreed-upon question:
> "What is the evidence that our students are able to reflect on their
> learning?" The science teacher brought several samples of student
> work to the group and expressed dissatisfaction with her students'
> ability to reflect on their learning. She noticed that they were most
> likely to describe what they learned based on the topic under
> consideration ("I learned a lot about ants and their habits.") or the
> methods they used to learn something ("I looked at websites my
> teacher suggested.") Her colleagues made some suggestions about
> how she could help her students focus on "how," rather than
> "what" they learned, and on themselves as learners.
>
> Following the discussion of her students' work, a more experi-
> enced language arts teacher presented a whole-class reflection,
> which followed a unit in which the students wrote persuasive
> letters to the mayor of their town. In their reflections on what was
> difficult and easy for them in writing the letter, students grappled
> with the issue of why it was hard to think about an issue from the
> mayor's point of view and why doing so mattered in writing an
> effective persuasive letter.
>
> As the science teacher read the students' reflections, which
> were posted on newsprint, she had an insight into her own frame of
> reference about reflection: "I guess I really did not have a clear
> sense of what I was asking the kids to do. I haven't had to do a lot
> of this kind of reflecting myself."

In the vignette, the science teacher realizes that she was unclear about
what she was asking students to do, in part because her own experiences
in education had not required the kind of reflection she observed students
carrying out in her colleague's class. The courage to acknowledge and ex-
press an insight about one's own learning and teaching is critical to un-
covering beliefs and misconceptions, but the experience may be unsettling

because, as might have been in the case of this teacher, it has to do with questions of identity, pondered in public.

Uncovering Hidden Assumptions

In their study *How the Way We Talk Can Change the Way We Work*, Kegan and Lahey (2001) argue that the reason change seldom occurs, either on an individual or organizational level, is that we do not uncover the hidden assumptions that bolster our fear of change and that indeed work to sustain our behavior in its present mode. The authors suggest that, to act on a commitment to change ("I want to become a more reflective teacher"), we must understand and articulate these assumption(s)—often central to our identity and status—that may keep us from acting. For example, the science teacher in the previously mentioned vignette may have feared that she would never be good at fostering her own students' reflection because her own education had been so different. Kegan and Lahey (2001) suggest that once such assumptions and fears are expressed, they are less frightening and we are more capable of reframing and acting on our commitments to change. They also suggest that an added problem is faulty language and assumptions about change: We approach change as a "problem" to be "overcome" through resolve and willpower—the "New Year's resolution" approach to change. They suggest that unless we understand our reasons for fearing change, "willpower" will not be enough to effect real change.

Dealing with the emotional aspects of inquiry and achieving true transformative learning is made more difficult because the norms of collegiality in most schools do not include raising difficult issues. Inquiry group members may choose not to deal with issues of consequence to their participants. In a study of action research groups over a 6-year time period, researchers found that uncontroversial topics were chosen rather than those that might shake up the established instructional routines of individual classrooms (Allen & Calhoun, 1998). In the authors' experience, research into instructional issues was seldom undertaken: "[I]t was much safer to study student behavior in the lunchroom than to study individual classroom instructional practices for their effects on student achievement" (p. 707). Groups dealing with such relatively uncomplex topics are unlikely to contribute significantly to change on an individual or school level.

Establishing Group Norms

In an account of a classroom in which learning for understanding takes place, the National Research Council study, cited earlier, emphasizes the need to create a community through establishing clear norms of behavior and expectations for learning: "In such a community, students might help one another solve problems by building on each other's knowledge, asking questions to clarify explanations, and suggesting avenues that might move the group toward its goal" (Brown & Campione, 1994). Both cooperation in problem solving (Evans, 1989; Newstead & Evans, 1995) and argumentation (Goldman, 1994; Habermas, 1990; Kuhn, 1991; Moshman, 1995a, 1995b; Salmon & Zeitz, 1995; Youniss & Damon, 1992) among students in such an intellectual community "enhance cognitive development" (National Research Council [NRC], 2000, p. 25). We suggest that teachers need the same kind of community, one that establishes clear norms and fosters intellectual engagement and excitement that is carried back to the classroom. Such an environment would be emotionally "safe" and supportive and foster reflection and the kind of transformative learning that teachers must undergo to change their practice. Over time, in such an environment, our seventh-grade science teacher could become a more reflective learner and hence more capable of structuring such learning experiences with her students.

ORGANIZATIONAL LEARNING AND INQUIRY

Imagine a school that loses all its records but still retains its building and staff. Then imagine a school that retains the building and its records, but loses its staff. In the first instance, the school will be able to reconstitute itself in the way it was. In the second, it will be a new school. Why? Because a school exists in the mind of its staff, or more precisely in the "mental models" that people have of the school. The school that will be reproduced by the staff will reflect their mental model of what a school should be and how it should interact with students, parents, and the community as well as how staff and leaders should interact (Adapted to a school setting from D. H. Kim's example of a company, 1993).

Often the mental models that people have may not allow for the kind of development and growth that nurtures learning either among staff or students (Kim, 1993). Organizational theorists argue that "most organizations have shared assumptions that protect the status quo, preclude people from challenging others' troublesome or difficult qualities and characteristics, and provide silent assent to those attributions; hence, very little learning is possible" (p. 41).

What does it take to create a learning organization? What does it take for an entire school—not just a team or department—to be capable of changing for the benefit of its students and staff? Although there is a great deal of new theory and empirical research on how people learn, which is beginning to inform education and professional development, there is much less research on how schools learn. Indeed, organizations in general present a curious paradox to researchers (Argyris & Schön, 1978):

> Organizations are not merely collections of individuals, yet there are no organizations without such collections. Similarly, organizational learning is not merely individual learning, yet organizations learn only through the experience and actions of individuals. What then are we to make of organizational learning? And what is an organization that it may learn? (cited in Kim, 1993, p. 40)

Organizational theorists argue that there are two forms of learning in an organization: operational and conceptual. Operational learning has to do with technical know-how and procedures; conceptual learning involves thinking about why things are done and sometimes challenging the prevailing conditions; this involves identifying and articulating tacit images of how things work or how people characteristically behave. Once these have been acknowledged, it is possible to develop a new framework or mental model for an organization. Clearly both operational and conceptual learning are needed to make an organization functional; these two types of learning can be seen as paralleling the "facts/information" and "concepts" of individual learning.

Organizational learning is dependent on people making mental models explicit in order to develop new, shared models. However, organizational learning is very often limited to operational learning and may be impervious to conceptual learning, without which substantial improvements are not possible. For example, a school that restructures itself into teams or houses without affecting the values and beliefs about instruction and all students' ability to learn leaves intact the heart of the educational enterprise and does not challenge the mental models that underpin them. It is for this reason that Sarason (1996), Fullan (1999), King and Newmann (2000), and other school improvement researchers talk about "reculturing," not "restructuring" schools to ensure organizational learning.

Reculturing in a school involves the surfacing of mental models of the school, not by individuals but by an entire school community. To make them explicit, a school would have to involve its staff in discussions in which they are able to examine their unspoken assumptions about students, teaching, and a range of other relevant issues. For example, staff may uncover contrasting beliefs about students' abilities based on their individual perspectives on their families, their social class, gender, race/ethnicity, or disabling conditions. As faculty they may decide that they need to explore these differences and develop greater understanding about their students and their students' families and communities. They may develop new mental models to reflect this new understanding and new language to inform action.

In order to unravel such mental models and reframe them, school-wide inquiry is essential. Michael Fullan cautions that, while we now have examples of schools that have successfully done this work, we still do not have enough research on precisely what such schools do "on Monday" and over time to accomplish a substantial change in students' learning (Fullan, 1999). King and Newmann (2000), for example, describe high schools with students from low-income families in which what they call "high professional community" is the norm. While teachers in these schools have conducted school-wide inquiry into teaching and learning on an ongoing basis in order to improve student learning for a number of years, the process by which they became "high professional communities" is not clear.

In the next section, we describe lessons learned from an elementary school that undertook various forms of collaborative inquiry over a 5-year period in order to improve the achievement of its diverse student body. This case offers a window into how the culture and values of schools practicing inquiry develop.

THE CULTURE AND VALUES OF INQUIRING SCHOOLS

In the process of reculturing a school, inquiry into teacher and student work is critical. Laura Stokes (2001) provides a vivid picture of an elementary school in California that undertook a 5-year process of inquiry. The process was one that led to school-wide engagement of staff in a variety of inquiry groups—some school-wide and mandated, others voluntary and focused on teachers' questions. The result was a substantial improvement in students' learning—an outcome that was sought but remained elusive during the first 3 years of the staff's work.

The work was funded initially by a state-wide initiative that focused on staff development to conduct inquiry into student achievement that would determine the "extent to which all students are habitually experiencing positive outcomes." Complementing this was a district-wide initiative that encouraged voluntary groups to inquire into questions that would close the racial gap in student achievement.

Types of Inquiry at the School

Three types of inquiry were conducted over a 5-year period. These included:

> *School-wide inquiry into test data and student work*: All staff participated in developing performance benchmarks, creating and administering assessments, and scoring them. They discussed and evaluated student work and made data regarding student scores available to the entire staff.
>
> *Biweekly grade-level action research teams*: Staff participated biweekly in individual action research teams on their grade levels. Teams developed their own questions for investigation, and each team was required to make its findings public to the entire school; and
>
> *Voluntary groups reflecting on practice*: Small, voluntary support groups met to reflect critically on their members' practices, with an emphasis on the beliefs and values that underlay them. There was no obligation to report to the entire staff.

In her analysis of what happened over 5 years, Stokes (2001) points to what the various forms of inquiry enabled teachers to learn and do and what they did not. For example, the school-wide inquiry enabled staff to discover that their students' reading was not as good as they had assumed; with time, the reading scores improved on average, but gaps between students of color and others persisted. What the school-wide work did not foster was a deep understanding of the nature of difficulties that struggling students were experiencing or the teaching strategies that could successfully address them. For this, a different form of inquiry was needed involving action research into individual classrooms by grade level and later voluntary study groups, in which teachers probed deeply into their own beliefs about students' ability to learn.

At the end of 5 years, this school began to see results in closing the gap between the literacy levels of White students and African American and Latino students. Although teachers' inquiry into school practices contributing to the racial gap in students' learning led to some painful confrontations and insights, addressing this gap would not have been possible unless staff had held some shared core values regarding inquiry and collective responsibility for student learning. These values and other key elements to fostering a culture of inquiry in a school are discussed briefly below. They are: an inquiry stance; collective responsibility for learning; mastery of the technical aspects of inquiry; a variety of inquiry methods in use; leadership and resources for inquiry; time for sustaining inquiry over time; and trust.

An Inquiry Stance

In her discussion of lessons learned, Stokes (2001) points to the shared core values and techniques that supported inquiry in the school. On the one hand, without the willingness to call into question customary ways of doing things, not only procedures or operations, but also core values and beliefs, inquiry will not surface and challenge existing mental models. Without this challenge, organizational learning cannot occur. Stokes calls this "critical will." Other researchers cited in this chapter make similar points. Cochran-Smith and Lytle (1999), for example, contrast an inquiry stance to one in which teachers rely either on external researchers for expertise or on the expertise of the most effective teachers. They argue that the highly contextual nature of useful knowledge about teaching makes it essential for teachers to collaborate in inquiring into their own practices and their impact on students and to make this knowledge available to other staff.

Collective Responsibility for Learning

In addition to critical will, Stokes (2001) points to the "collectivity of effort" that was involved based on the teachers' sense that they were collectively responsible for student learning. Much school improvement literature suggests that until the staff becomes collectively responsible for student learning, it will not improve (Fullan, 1999; King & Newmann, 2000). Thus, when one teacher or a group of teachers become expert in something that positively affects students' learning, this alone will not foster overall improvement in student learning unless the knowledge is widely shared and discussed; that is, unless it becomes part of the school's learning.

Mastery of the Technical Aspects of Inquiry

Inquiry work requires the development of technical capacity to study and understand data, use protocols for reviewing student work or examining instructional practices, and establish norms of behavior. These technical aspects of inquiry are dealt with in later chapters in this book. They often require the expertise of outside organizations and individuals who provide assistance in organizing and facilitating the inquiry work. Outside groups or individuals also help sustain the work by providing problem-solving strategies for inquiry groups encountering difficulties and by offering moral support to these groups as they address the challenges of reform work. The case studies in this book provide examples of such technical and moral support and how teachers used them to accommodate their schools' needs.

A Variety of Inquiry Methods Used

Stokes (2001) argues that the fact that the school engaged in different types of inquiry—whole-school, grade-level action research, and voluntary groups focused on instruction and beliefs about students' abilities—over 5 years allowed for interplay between what individuals learned about their own classrooms and their students and what they learned about school-wide practices. It allowed teachers to become more expert both about their school as a whole and about their individual classrooms and teams. This suggests that there must be an interplay between different types of inquiry that fosters individual, team, and whole-school learning and provides the basis for making school-wide change. The case studies in the second part of this book illustrate this interplay among the various types of inquiry.

Leadership and Resources for Inquiry

In schools that improve through inquiry, leadership by principals and teachers is critical to developing and sustaining the work. McLaughlin and Talbert (2001) analyze the types of leadership that helped high schools improve learning outcomes for students through teacher innovation and inquiry into student work and instruction. In these schools, principals focused on teaching and learning that addressed student needs and built on their strengths; garnered community resources; mediated between the district or state and the teachers when needed; and encouraged frequent use of external resources to improve teaching. All the schools in the case studies in this book had leadership that encouraged and supported inquiry, as did the school that Stokes (2001) studied over 5 years. In some situations when school leadership changed, district leadership provided the support for the continuation of inquiry.

Time for Inquiry and Sustaining Inquiry over Time

The inquiry process in the school studied by Stokes emphasizes the need to integrate time for inquiry into the school day, rather than burden teachers with additional after-school commitments. Doing this also recognizes the centrality of inquiry to improving instruction and student learning. Chapter 2 describes schools that have successfully integrated time for inquiry into the day.

Current timetables for improvement in student outcomes demand almost immediate results, at least on standardized tests. The inquiry described in this book requires several years to develop and mature. The school described by Stokes (2001) was involved in a 5-year effort to improve student outcomes through a variety of approaches to inquiry. Other studies of teacher inquiry groups have found that it often takes 2 years of ongoing meetings before teachers feel fully comfortable in discussing difficult issues (Clark, 2001). It is likely that different teams of teachers and schools will have different trajectories in developing collaborative inquiry groups based on their history and experience, but inquiry involving deep thinking, trust, and negotiation of differences that translates into important school and classroom changes cannot be accomplished quickly.

Trust

Underlying all the values that Stokes (2001) and others have outlined is trust—trust between principal and teachers, among teachers, between teachers and parents, and between teachers and students. Deborah Meier (2002) has argued eloquently about the need for trusting relationships in schools as the basis of good and continuously improving educational practice. In particular, she points to the profound need of parents to trust a school and its staff, to believe that their children will not be harmed and will learn in ways that support their development and their preparation for the future. This parental need for trust in schools places a tremendous responsibility on teachers and school leaders to maintain open communication with parents and to invite and welcome their interest and involvement in their children's education. Similarly, trust among teachers is the essential basis for the types of collaboration that Stokes (2001) describes and that we describe in this book. Trust among teachers makes it possible to surface and discuss differences, such as those based on race, gender, age, and experience. Stokes (2001) and Meier (2002) suggest that surfacing and understanding such differences allows a school to move forward rather than remain frozen in dysfunctional mental models that accommodate inertia and incompetence.

Recent research by Anthony Bryk and Barbara Schneider (2002) confirms what most teachers would intuit—namely, that schools in which trust exists are more likely to improve than schools without it. Drawing on the literature of "social capital," they argue that when trusting relationships develop and are sustained, schools are more likely to have the dense social relationships that support collaboration and collective effort to improve over time.

For their study, Bryk and Schneider (2002) analyzed school achievement data from 100 Chicago schools with the greatest improvements in reading and mathematics between 1991 and 1996 and 100 schools with little or no improvement. Schools with trusting relationships had a one in two chance of improving, while those with weak relationships had a one in seven chance of doing so. They also found that schools with weak relationships that improved did strengthen their relationships over time. Even controlling for such factors as high poverty rates, the statistical link between trust and school improvement is strong.

We do not know the extent to which the improving schools that Bryk and Schneider (2002) studied also developed collaborative inquiry groups and how inquiry contributed to the improvement of student learning. But it is clear that collaborative inquiry cannot occur without "relational trust" and that it can, in turn, deepen that trust.

Conclusion

Earlier in this chapter we presented a vignette of a teacher who found that her students had difficulty reflecting on their work and became aware through her inquiry group that she had not been asked to reflect on her own learning as a student. In her case study, Stokes (2001) described teachers who felt deeply affronted when others challenged their practices as potentially contributing to the racial achievement gap between students. These stories, and the stories in later chapters of this book, point to the emotional work of improving teaching and to its intellectual complexity (Hargreaves, 1998). Nevertheless, when a school embraces an inquiry stance—that is, when it assumes that all teachers will engage in inquiry and that it will be done in a supportive and collaborative manner, and when trust is developed and nurtured in schools, then challenges, although painful, may also in time be accepted as part of the process of learning, growing, and improving.

These stories also point to the broad social and moral purposes of schooling. Because education is concerned with human development of both students and teachers and the maximizing of human potential regardless of social and economic barriers, it is not possible to genuinely address educational issues without engaging in debate, surfacing preconceptions, and reframing what we already know in terms of new information, new concepts, and new purposes. This is an ongoing, emotionally and intellectually engaging process, which for some schools, such as those described in this book or the one that Stokes (2001) described, becomes a norm.

In a recent interview (Sparks, 2003), Michael Fullan argues that if we as a country were to attain a policy environment in which "informed professional judgment" (p. 56) by teachers became the norm, then teachers would have to "see themselves as scientists who continuously develop their intellectual and investigative effectiveness" (p. 57). The process must be rooted in collaborative inquiry, since all knowledge, whether from the outside or from within the school, needs to be processed to become usable knowledge. In Fullan's words, in organizational settings, "information becomes knowledge through a social process, and knowledge becomes wisdom through sustained interaction"(p. 57).

Just as there will never be simple answers to the complexities of teaching, so there will never be a single or simple approach for conducting inquiry groups that will be appropriate for all teachers and all schools. As Cochran-Smith and Lytle (1999) suggest, inquiry is a "stance," and schools like the one that Stokes (2001) and McLaughlin and Talbert (2001) studied, as well as the schools described in this book, provide instructive lessons about how to conduct inquiry into student and teacher work, as well as the decision points and the potential benefits, contributions, and limitations of each type of inquiry.

It is certainly easier to mandate that teachers follow a scripted curriculum than to develop effective groups in which teachers examine their daily practices in the light of pressing student needs and realities, especially within a high-stakes accountability policy environment. It takes time, the scarcest commodity in schools; "critical will"; and courage. Although there are no assurances that inquiry will yield the results that teachers, the public, and policymakers want, it is only through inquiry into teacher practice and student learning that teachers will become proficient at the inquiry process, learn better what forms of inquiry suit their schools, and develop the knowledge base that can improve their students' learning.

Chapter 2

Critical Considerations for Starting Inquiry

What is the purpose of homework, or recess—or school itself, for that matter? Ask five teachers and you're likely to get (at least!) five different answers. While we might all agree that having a clearly defined purpose for engaging in something as important as collaborative inquiry is essential, we're also bound to admit that we often undertake significant endeavors before we have absolute clarity of purpose.

In the case of collaborative inquiry, this lack of a clear and commonly held purpose is usually not attributable to resistance on the part of the teachers participating or lack of vision on the part of principals. Instead, it signals a quality of inquiry that is at once fascinating and frustrating. In collaborative inquiry, unlike more traditional forms of staff development such as workshops or courses, purposes are not fixed, but dynamic.

This dynamic quality suggests that, whatever the group's stated purpose—for example, assessing a particular instructional strategy or understanding and addressing issues of equity within the school—the purpose will respond to and be reshaped by the group's ongoing experiences with inquiry and the deepening understandings that emerge from that inquiry. At times, the purpose may even be reshaped in response to a group's frustration that a focus question or approach to collecting data seems to be leading to a dead end.

This chapter begins with a discussion of how purposes for inquiry are defined in different ways in different school settings. It goes on to consider some of the key decisions principals and those involved in the inquiry—either in supporting it or directly taking part in it—must make in getting inquiry going and sustaining it. We treat purposes and decisions together because they continually affect one another: The purposes you start out with, however broad, affect the decisions you make; and the decisions you make affect your evolving definition of purpose.

In inquiry groups, purposes find their truest expression in the question or questions the group members choose to explore. So, for example, a group or teacher asking, "How can I assess my students' work in a way that will help motivate them rather than just serving as reward or punishment?" is purposefully engaging in a reexamination of assessment practice, one that may contribute to new assessment strategies that will help motivate students to perform at higher levels. A group asking, "Why are African American and Latino students in the school disproportionately represented among those reading below grade level?" is, similarly purposefully, "auditing" the distribution of resources and opportunities within the school in order to create more equitable conditions for all students.

Defining and Refining Purpose

The process by which groups develop, test, and revise questions represents a continual "repurposing" by which they become clearer and clearer about why they are engaging in inquiry. This process takes time—often several months of meetings, and sometimes even a year of work together. This is not to say that all, or even most, inquiry groups start out with a blank slate when it comes to purpose. In many situations, administrators frame a purpose for the inquiry before groups are formed and inquiry begins. Some examples of purposes include improving instruction, assessing the effectiveness of a curriculum or an instructional practice, and investigating issues of equity.

This initial, and often broad, framing of purpose can be seen as an opening of the "space" in which inquiry can take place and an invitation to teachers, and others, to take part—to come to the table. The process may begin with the principal and other administrators taking stock of current school goals and practices and identifying areas for improvement or investigation—as described in Chapter 6—in which the principal encourages an inquiry group to investigate a mandated literacy curriculum. In many cases the administration involves the faculty in the framing process—for example, by forming a planning team, as described in Chapter 3, or getting input from teachers (and others) at key points in the evolution of inquiry, as described in Chapter 5. Sometimes the initiative may come from the district level, as described in Chapter 4.

Depending on the school context, culture, and leadership, some groups might start with a more open-ended sense of purpose, trusting that, over time, it will become more defined. One way that schools have begun to consider purposes for inquiry is to bring to the surface some of the questions that teachers and others in the school have—whether or not they have been articulated. When teachers are invited to step back and reflect on their practice, they discover that they have important questions about how their students learn, the content of the curriculum, effective means of providing instruction and assessing student learning, how to achieve district or state standards, and so on. For example, an inquiry group of middle-grade teachers began by identifying the individual questions of the participants. When it became clear, over the first few meetings, that most of the teachers' questions, in one way or another, concerned the teaching of writing, the group developed an "umbrella question" about teaching writing across the curriculum. Investigating and developing effective strategies for writing instruction across grade levels became this group's purpose over the following 3 years.

Whether explicit or open-ended at the start—and there are many shades between—the defining and refining of purpose should be done with the goals of promoting student understanding and supporting student learning. As obvious as this commitment appears to be, it is easy for a group to find itself discussing organizational, curricular, and even instructional issues, without connecting them directly to evidence of student learning.

Reflecting on and Communicating Purpose

Having a continually developing sense of purpose does not mean inquiry groups shouldn't be able to articulate their purpose for themselves and others. In fact, because purpose in inquiry groups is dynamic and responsive to classroom and school realities, it becomes even more important for inquiry groups to reflect regularly on their stated, or understood, purpose. Groups often do this by allocating time in meetings to address questions such as:

- What do we now want to learn about or understand better?
- Is/are our question(s) the right one(s) to help us get there?
- How is what we're learning affecting, or likely to affect, the teaching and learning in our classrooms and the school?

When these discussions are documented, as we illustrate in a later section, a group is able to trace the developing arc of its inquiry over time. Documentation can provide a particularly effective touchstone for a group's reflection on its own learning. It can also allow a group to communicate its process and learning to others in the school community and beyond. (See Chapter 4 for another set of questions that groups ask in reflecting on their inquiry.)

Lessons about Purpose

We close our discussion of purposes with some crucial lessons that have come from the inquiry groups with which we have worked in a variety of settings:

- *Variation.* Schools are unique, in terms of the community they serve, district and state context, history of professional development initiatives, and culture. One purpose will not fit all. It is critical for principals and others involved in defining the purpose for inquiry to look for consistency with other valued school practices and rituals, as well as look out for areas of possible conflict, contradiction, or overload.
- *Perspectives.* In framing purposes for inquiry, administrators should involve the voices of teachers and other likely participants. Often, school or district administrators who do not participate in groups will have a conceptualization of the purposes for the work that differs from that of participants. Discussion of purpose should not end once the work is started, but rather be revisited frequently in group discussion and meetings with leaders.
- *Relevance.* Purposes need to be continually checked for their relevance to student learning and student understanding. It's easy to "hug the shore" in talking about teaching practice or curriculum materials without making the critical link to student understanding, performance, or achievement.
- *Serendipity.* It is important to recognize that inquiry is not a linear process—finding the shortest line between two points. When practiced seriously over time, inquiry leads both to intended or predictable outcomes and unintended, even serendipitous, outcomes. Both kinds of outcomes can affect the shape and direction of future inquiry.
- *Get going!* Purposes evolve or become clearer over time. While a school or group may begin with a fairly broad purpose (for example, to improve instructional practice), it often pays to get started with inquiry before purposes are fully articulated—heeding Michael Fullan's (1993) maxim about school change: "Ready, Fire, Aim!"

A "TABLE" OF DECISION POINTS

A shared, continually deepening understanding of purpose for inquiry will help administrators and participants make key decisions about the form that inquiry will take. Many of these critical "decision points" will occur in the early stages of planning inquiry; others will come up during inquiry and will affect how the process is started and sustained, and with which outcomes.

School (and sometimes district) administrators, especially principals, play critical roles in making decisions, but, as we have seen with framing purposes, making productive decisions requires active participation by all those engaged in the endeavor, including teachers in the group(s) as well as administrators who may or may not be active participants. The process will also benefit from the perspectives that outside partners can supply—for example, coaches or facilitators from a university or partner organization.

Decision points don't usually follow a single identifiable time line or trajectory: Some are predictable; others will emerge only once the work begins to take shape. In this chapter, we highlight some of the major decision categories that schools and districts face as they implement collaborative inquiry. For each, we offer some examples of how real people in real schools have made decisions, how their decisions connected to the established purposes, and discuss some of the benefits and trade-offs that their decisions entailed.

To organize these categories of decisions, we use the metaphor of a table. While inquiry happens in different places in the school, it often involves educators gathered around a table in a faculty room or school library. While the initial framing of purpose(s) serves as an invitation to take part in inquiry—to come to the table—it doesn't answer all the questions about what goes on once you're there. Our metaphorical table of decision points has four "legs," each representing a key set of questions that serve to support collaborative inquiry. These questions are presented in outline form below and addressed in greater detail in the sections that follow:

What Is on the Table?

- What will the groups focus on?
- What questions will the group focus on?
- What kinds of data will the group look at?
  —School or district-generated data
  —Student and teacher work samples
  —Other data

Who Is at the Table?

- How are groups formed?
- Will participation be required or voluntary?
- Will groups be formed by or across grade level or discipline?

What Happens at the Table?

- How do groups set norms for inquiry?
- How do groups use inquiry cycles to map inquiry?
- How do groups use protocols to structure inquiry?
- How is inquiry facilitated?
- How is inquiry documented?

How Is the Table Supported?

- How are resources, especially time, provided for inquiry?
- What role do partnerships play in building capacity for inquiry?
- What incentives are offered to participants?
- How is the value of the inquiry communicated to others in the school community?
- How are adjustments made to support continued inquiry?
- How does the work grow and expand?

In the next section, we will look more closely at each of these parts of the inquiry table. The order in which we treat them is somewhat arbitrary; particular decisions from any of the four categories may come up at any point in the process and, of course, some decisions will straddle more than one category.

What Is on the Table?

Schools are not alone in living the "unexamined life." But they may be uniquely structured to produce more data about their performance (in terms of student learning) with fewer opportunities for the participants in the enterprise—teachers and administrators—to examine, reflect on, and learn from those data in order to improve performance.

Imagine all the tables that would be required to hold just the student and teacher work of one typical school week. Now add the results from standardized tests and the data routinely collected by schools and districts. Add to that the other kinds of formal and informal research that take place in schools—carried out by individual teachers or administrators, by university researchers, or by parent or community groups—including surveys, interviews, and observations.

With that image in mind, consider how much time the typical teacher has to look closely at data, discuss them with colleagues, and make appropriate adjustments in his or her instruction and assessment. In most cases, it's little or none. The point is not, of course, for an inquiry group to try to wade through all this information. Rather, in thinking about the purposes for inquiry, the group should be encouraged to consider how best to "sample" the data and determine how the samples can be used to answer the important questions they have framed for inquiry.

The frame for examining data is provided by the questions that the groups (or individuals within it) pose about teaching and learning. Once a group or school has initially developed its individual or group questions, the process of identifying what to bring to the table usually becomes somewhat clearer. In the next section, we consider how groups identify and develop inquiry questions. In the sections that follow, we discuss three broad categories of data: (1) data generated by the school or district, (2) samples of students' work and teachers' work, and (3) other data, including classroom observations, video from other classrooms, and published research studies.

While practically everything that a teacher or group brings to the table (except the snacks!) can be considered data, these categories may be useful in helping groups think about those data that are most likely to help them address their questions and purposes.

Putting Questions on the Table

Before addressing the kinds of data that are put out on the table, schools and groups typically devote considerable time to determining what kinds of questions will guide the inquiry. These questions not only help articulate the group's purpose, as discussed above, but function as a lens or filter in selecting (i.e., sampling) the materials that are brought to the table.

In some teacher inquiry groups whose purpose it is to better understand how their practice supports student learning, teachers frame questions that are unique to the individual teachers in the group. Inquiry groups using the Evidence Process, developed by Project Zero, often found it helpful to use a simple "protocol," or set of steps (more about protocols appears later in this chapter), to guide their conversations about potential inquiry questions. The protocol, which consists of three questions, gives teachers a starting place, or prompt, for thinking about possible inquiry questions as well as a tool the group can use to "vet" candidate questions before collecting data to address them. The three questions are:

- Is the teacher's question personally important?
- Is it relevant to classrooms beyond his or her own?
- Is it connected to student learning?

If these questions are answered affirmatively, the group may also consider whether the question seems too broad or too narrow to pursue over a significant period of time (a semester or entire year) and the kinds of "evidence," or data, the asking teacher might begin to gather from her or his classroom to present to the group. In groups that use this protocol, some of the questions that have emerged are: How can I help students to improve their writing in math? How do [early elementary] children learn from (or during) play? and Do I talk too much [in teaching writing]?

While these are all questions generated by individual teachers, groups tend to develop a collective and collegial "ownership" of questions they find relevant and compelling. This contributes to learning for both the asking (presenting) teacher and others in the group. At times, groups intentionally develop collective questions, as well as, or in place of, individual questions; for example, What does a "learning expedition" look like? (see Chapter 5), How do students learn to practice the "golden rule" [in early elementary grades]?, and How are students able to think critically about their own learning?

Data Generated by the School or District

This category includes information that is either already, or could easily be, collected, compiled, or sorted. For example, schools and districts maintain a great deal of data, including student scores on standardized tests, attendance, graduation and dropout rates, number of referrals to special services, percentage of students enrolled in or passing individual courses, and number of suspensions. These data are often quantitative, and sometimes disaggregated, or broken down, for example, by race, ethnicity, language, socioeconomic status, and gender.

Schools and groups asking questions about how well their students—as individuals, groups, or subgroups—are achieving identified learning goals or standards may choose to analyze standardized test scores in math or results on a school-wide writing assessment, focusing on specific items that assess student performance. These kinds of data may be particularly useful to put on the table when a group has questions about equity. For example, a school may be exploring how many of its students—and which ones (in terms of race, gender, or special status)—are taking algebra, often considered an important benchmark for admission to and success in college.

Samples of Student and Teacher Work

This category refers to materials, sometimes called "artifacts," gathered from the classroom that represent the actual teaching and learning that takes place there. These data exist whether or not a systematic inquiry exists to "tap" them. They are found on bulletin boards, in student folders and portfolios, and on teachers' desks and planning books. This almost infinitely broad category can be broken down into two subcategories: samples of student work and samples of teacher work. Of course, there are many other possible artifacts—for example, letters that teachers send home to parents—but teacher inquiry groups most commonly focus on materials from students' and teachers' work since these represent the daily currency of teaching and learning.

Student Work. The forms that student work take encompass an almost infinite variety. Some very broad categories of student work are:

- written, visual, and three-dimensional pieces (essays, posters, presentations, reports, problem sets, etc.)
- drafts and finished pieces
- individual and collaborative pieces
- performances (exhibitions, skits, etc.)
- process-oriented work (class or group discussion, conferences with the teacher, etc.)

The last two categories of less tangible work can be challenging to collect in a form that can be presented to a group; however, video and audio taping can, with careful planning (and, sometimes, help from an outside partner), provide access to these data.

Teacher Work. The ways in which teachers support student learning are as varied as the kinds of work that students complete. Some of the forms of teacher work that might be reviewed include:

- unit, project, and lesson plans
- assessment instruments (rubrics, checklists, etc.)
- resources that teachers create for students (time lines, models, etc.)
- published curriculum materials

Selecting Work to Present. In identifying samples of student work, teachers often select pieces from students who are struggling or students who "puzzle" them—in either case, they are hoping that the perspectives of other group members will help them better understand and deal with these challenging cases. In choosing teacher work to bring to the table, participants might select an assignment or scoring rubric with which they are dissatisfied. (This is not to say that inquiry cannot profit from looking at an assignment or sample of student work that went particularly well; as groups often discover, these successful pieces, too, benefit from "fine-tuning" and contribute to the group's learning.)

Teachers often bring a set of data that includes both samples of student work and the assignment and/or scoring criteria (for example, a rubric) that relates to them. A group engaged in improving its curriculum and instruction in a particular area—such as writing across the curriculum—is likely to bring samples of student writing from different subjects, along with the writing prompts and rubrics that teachers have created or adapted. A group that is focused on a more specific learning goal or standard is likely to bring copies of that standard, an assignment that is intended to address it, and student work samples representing various levels of success. A school looking at issues of equity might look both at school- and district-generated data, as described above, as well as what students say about themselves and their classes in written reflective pieces, on surveys, or in class discussions.

In making decisions about what work to bring—teachers' or students' (or both), which students' work, how much work, and so forth—participants should be guided by the group's purpose(s) and its questions. It may also be helpful to consult with an experienced facilitator or coach. Table 2.1 is offered as another resource. In addition to the kinds of student and/or teacher work that is brought to address different kinds of questions, it also suggests one or more "protocols" to use in looking at the work. Protocols are an important tool for inquiry treated later in this chapter (for more information about the protocols, see Allen, 1998; McDonald et al., 2003; Project Zero, 2001).

While it may appear to be a daunting task to figure out how to select from these ever-expanding pools of data, with time groups and the individual teachers in them develop skills and strategies for sampling through trial and error and by reflecting together on their data collection process as part of their meetings.

Other Data

This third category comprises data that must be compiled or created in response to the group's question(s) (unlike classroom-generated and school- and/or district-generated data, which exist independently of an inquiry group's work). Research studies can be *inward*-looking—that is, focused on the participating teacher's or teachers' classroom(s); or *outward*-looking—exploring classrooms or other educational settings outside of the

Table 2.1. Selecting Work to Present

Question deals with:	Student work might include:	Teacher work might include:	Protocols that may be used:
Effectiveness of a task, assignment, or prompt	Multiple samples (3–5) at different levels of achievement; drafts and finished pieces	Copies of the task, assignment, or prompt	Tuning Protocol; Reflecting on Learning Expedition Plans (See Chapter 5)
Individual student's strengths, deficits, understanding, etc.	Single sample of work or multiple samples from individual student	(Focus is not on teacher work, but relevant pieces may be brought as references)	Collaborative Assessment Conference; Modified Collaborative Assessment Conference (See Chapter 5)
Effectiveness of an assessment tool	Multiple samples (3–5) at different levels of achievement	Copies of rubric, scoring guide, or criteria	Tuning Protocol
Alignment of curriculum, instruction, or assessment with standard	Multiple samples (3–5) at different levels of achievement	Copies of standard and curriculum task and/or assessment instrument	Standards in Practice; Tuning Protocol
Teaching problems or dilemmas	(Samples of student work as appropriate to illustrate problem/dilemma)	Written/oral description of problem/dilemma; other documents as appropriate	Consultancy
Equity issues	Class set or samples from students in different subgroups (e.g., gender, race)	Copies of standard, task, assignment, rubric, etc. that relate to issue	Slice; Tuning Protocol; Consultancy

school. Some of the inward-looking methods of study that inquiry groups have found most rewarding and practical are: surveys; interviews; observations of individual students, classrooms, or peers; and teachers' journals or other forms for reflection. Outward-looking methods include analyses of reading from journals or books, or reviewing materials generated by research conducted by others.

Looking in. Teachers may at first be intimidated by the idea of conducting a survey or set of interviews, let alone observing a class of one of their colleagues. But while these methods take thoughtful planning, they do not have to be elaborate or intrusive. A survey can be as simple as asking students to jot down their thoughts about one or two questions. For example, a teacher in a high school inquiry group asked her students to respond to the following question: What constitutes a good learning experience? Interviews can be similarly easy to conduct. In one elementary school inquiry group, a teacher took advantage of a bus ride back from a field trip to ask several students about how they learn best. In Chapter 3, Elena Aguilar, a sixth-grade humanities teacher in Oakland, California, surveys her students about their attitudes toward reading, generating data that are closely connected to the focus of her inquiry.

Looking out. While classroom observation is a powerful method for addressing inquiry questions, it typically takes a bit more planning than surveys or interviews. A teacher being observed typically meets with the observers ahead of time to determine what they will look for. A post-observation meeting is planned to discuss what the observers saw and how that relates to the agreed-upon focus.

While most inquiry groups are focused on examining what happens within classrooms and the school as a whole, it is often helpful to bring in relevant ideas or examples from the outside. One way to do this is to decide on a common reading from a book or professional journal that relates to the group's question or purposes.

A trade-off sometimes comes up in using outside materials between safety and authenticity. Groups are often eager to see examples (especially on video) of other schools' or teachers' work, especially during the initial stages of their own work. It may feel safer than looking closely at their own work and that of their students, or they may feel the work from the outside is more advanced and provides a good model. However, they may also find that the resulting conversations feel somewhat more abstract than when they focus on their own students and classrooms.

Looking Both Ways. Outward-looking research may be most powerful when it complements or provides a foundation for some of the inward-looking methods discussed above, as well as looking at school-, district-, or classroom-generated data. Viewing videos from other schools, for example, has been effective in practicing classroom observation skills and in thinking about how to offer useful feedback to peers. In Chapter 4, teachers at Maxson Middle School begin by looking at samples of work from other schools before presenting pieces from their own classrooms. In Chapter 6, teachers on the Sheltered English team at Melrose Elementary School begin their inquiry into a new literacy curriculum by looking carefully at the curriculum guide in light of their existing practices, then move to trying some of the practices and collecting and sharing samples of student work and observations from their own classrooms.

Who Is at the Table?

While the potential number of combinations of teachers within a school may not be quite as staggering as the possibilities for data, it is still significant, even in a small school. In putting together groups, administrators face many decisions—each bringing possible trade-offs.

How Are Groups Formed? (Or, How Did I Get Here?)

Decisions made about who should be at the table, like other important decisions, should be consistent with the purpose(s) for inquiry. Two of the most important questions in beginning inquiry are:

- Should the inquiry group(s) be formed voluntarily or be mandated, that is, required by the school leadership?
- Should groups be homogenous or heterogeneous by grade level or discipline?

Mandating versus Volunteering? When teachers are allowed to choose inquiry as a form of professional development—and supported in practicing it—there is typically a greater chance that they will "buy into" the inquiry process. On the other hand, involving all teachers in the school as a key component of their professional development signals a seriousness of the school's commitment to inquiry and teacher professionalism.

If teachers are required to take part, the inquiry in which groups engage should be clearly tied to valued school-wide goals. For example, the principal of a new school who saw inquiry as a way to develop the school's curriculum and build a collaborative professional culture chose to involve all teachers, including student teachers, in regular inquiry group meetings (see Chapter 5).

Another model for making decisions about composing groups is to engage in a whole-school process of identifying the important issues or questions to be investigated. With agreement at the school level, inquiry groups can be formed around the questions identified, and teachers can choose which group to join. This is an example of how "what's on the table" (the questions), as the first decision, influences "who's at the table" (group composition). It is also possible for the groups to be selected by a principal or another administrator. When the "who" is assigned rather than voluntary, it is especially important for the "what" to be determined by the group, by allowing the participants to identify and work on the questions that matter to them.

Decisions about self-selection versus required (mandated) participation are not always as clear-cut as they may seem. In one elementary school that was initiating inquiry groups, the principal presented the entire faculty in a full-faculty meeting with the opportunity to join a group. He also spoke individually with teachers for whom he felt this would be a particularly well-timed opportunity to develop as teachers and leaders within the school community. He discouraged others who were already committed to a significant professional development program for the coming year. The following year, when the other program ended, some of these teachers chose to join the inquiry groups.

Whether a group self-selects or is assigned, principals and other leaders must find ways to communicate to the group that it has the responsibility and authority, in other words, "ownership," to determine the focus of its inquiry.

Up, Down, Narrow, or Wide? Should groups be composed within or across grade levels? By subject-area teachers or across the subject areas?

Certainly inquiry benefits from bringing multiple perspectives to the table. For this reason, inquiry groups have often been composed across grade level or subject area. Teachers who initially question the value of meeting with colleagues who teach at very different grade levels usually come to appreciate the benefits of hearing different perspectives on their work as well as understanding more about the teaching and learning that takes place at other levels. An early skepticism about what a high school English teacher can offer to an algebra teacher, and vice versa, is often overcome through the discovery that questions and feedback from outside a particular discipline, as well as from within it, can add to everyone's understanding of core issues of teaching and learning. Often the person from outside the discipline will notice something significant that the specialists take for granted or overlook.

However, there is also value in bringing together teachers (and others) who are all working with students at a particular age or developmental stage. For example, a high school instituting a new ninth-grade "house" program chose to involve all the teachers at that grade level in inquiry group meetings with the purpose of integrating the curriculum and developing an advisory system.

Similarly, when there are multiple representatives from the same subject or discipline in a group, it can have the effect of "pushing" the conversation deeper, especially when discussing strategies for teaching specific content-related concepts or skills. This may be more significant for middle school and high school groups, where teachers tend to be disciplinary specialists rather than generalists.

One middle school began by forming groups by subject areas. As it became clearer that the school, a relatively new one, needed to focus on its interdisciplinary curriculum and assessment practices, the decision was made by the principal and faculty representatives to meet across disciplines and focus on integrated projects. While most teachers agreed the change was beneficial, some of the math teachers experienced dissatisfaction stemming from the lost opportunity, in their view, to focus on questions related to their subject (see Chapter 5). As this story shows, one outcome of inquiry can be to highlight other staff development needs; for example, opportunities for disciplinary specialists to work together to plan curriculum or create assessments.

Other Questions of Composition. While the questions listed above, regarding who is at the table, represent major decision points for schools forming inquiry groups, several additional questions should be considered as well:

- *How big should the groups be?* There is no magic number for effective inquiry groups. By its nature, collaborative inquiry involves hearing the perspectives of others and being heard. This is difficult to do in groups much larger than ten; however, in groups smaller than five there may be too few perspectives to create the rich, layered discussions that inquiry groups value.
- *Who should be involved beyond "core" teachers?* It can be very productive to include specialists who typically fall outside the core curriculum in inquiry groups—for example, art and physical education teachers, counselors, and special education teachers. Their presence both broadens the range of perspectives at the table and helps to extend the reach of the group's inquiry across the school.
- *Should administrators be involved in the groups?* While it can be extremely valuable for a principal or assistant principal to be in a group, both for the perspective she or he offers and as an opportunity for her or him to learn from the others' perspectives, it may be constraining or intimidating to group members and impinge on their ownership of the process. It may help to review the purposes for

the inquiry group(s) and clarify that the administrator is not there in order to evaluate teachers' performance. Of course, the culture of the school and the administrator's relationship with faculty are also factors to consider in making this decision.

What Happens at the Table?

What happens at your family dinner table or happened at the table of your youth? Without noticing it, families tend to have a set of routines or rituals, some passed down from generation to generation, that usually lead to somewhat predictable outcomes, whether enjoyable or not. Experimenting with a new routine can sometimes promote conversations that are more pleasant, interesting, or humorous.

When teachers meet around a table they also follow routines and rituals—also partially "inherited." It may not be noticed, but these patterns often lead to discussions that are unfocused, rich in anecdotes but short on data or analysis, and too often negative about students, colleagues, and the school. This is not surprising, given the lack of time to meet with colleagues and, in general, the lack of practice in having purposeful, professional conversations that characterize the teaching profession.

In order to have constructive conversations, teachers and other professionals benefit from forms or structures that can help keep their conversations focused, productive, and positive. In considering how inquiry groups work, we will look at five aspects of that support: norms, inquiry cycles, protocols, facilitation, and documentation.

Setting Norms for Inquiry

Being explicit about norms for the group's work together is an important and often overlooked aspect of a group's work. Because participants are adults and professionals, it may be assumed that they can just come together and get down to work. However, it is critical to give serious thought and discussion not only to *why* they have come together—that is, purpose—but also *how* they will work together productively.

Some inquiry groups spend part of a first meeting creating a list of norms, or guidelines, by individually answering the question, What helps me learn best within a group?, then sharing these responses and compiling a list. Lists of norms often include points such as, Don't be afraid to ask the question, Monitor your "airtime" (how much you talk in the meetings), and Keep a sense of humor about our work.

Groups periodically revisit their set of norms to see if they are living up to them, and if it would help to add or revise one. Groups that work together over time often develop implicit norms; however, it can be useful periodically to make them explicit through discussion.

Using Inquiry Cycles to Map the Inquiry

Tools for inquiry help a group structure its meetings or the conversations that take place within these meetings. Inquiry cycles can provide groups with a tool for thinking about and planning for the major phases of—and activities that comprise—its inquiry process and how they will proceed through them most productively.

Groups may adapt or create a "cycle of inquiry" that provides a tentative map for its ongoing work together. These cycles are often represented graphically. The Gears Diagram in Figure 2.1 was used by schools in the Evidence Project (Project Zero, 2001) to give the participants a sense of what the big parts of their inquiry process were going to be—questions, "evidence" from classrooms (such as samples of student or teacher work), protocols to discuss the evidence (see below), and so on—and how they might relate to each other. Of course the actual process played out differently in different groups, but the diagram was a useful starting place for conversations about how the work might proceed and a reference point for reflecting on the process along the way.

Using Protocols to Structure Inquiry

Protocols are somewhat smaller in scope than inquiry cycles and usually describe a set of steps that a group will follow in a particular conversation. While it may feel somewhat unnatural at first (it is!) to use a protocol to structure a conversation, participants quickly realize that without an explicit structure, conversations about teaching and learning tend to drift, go in many directions at once, or become so abstract that they are unlikely to lead to any useful learning.

Protocols help participants explicitly distinguish between observations, interpretations, or evaluations of the data or events being examined and strategies for responding to them. While unstructured conversations tend to blur observations with evaluation or interpretation, separating out these different responses often provides opportunities for insights and collective construction of knowledge that otherwise might elude us.

Another reason for protocols is safety. For most teachers, at least initially, sharing work from their classroom with colleagues is an unusual and somewhat intimidating idea. The protocols provide a predictable, safe environment to open up teachers' (and students') work to inquiry. They help to keep the conversation focused on asking questions and sharing

Figure 2.1. Gears diagram

THE EVIDENCE PROCESS
("GEARS" DIAGRAM)

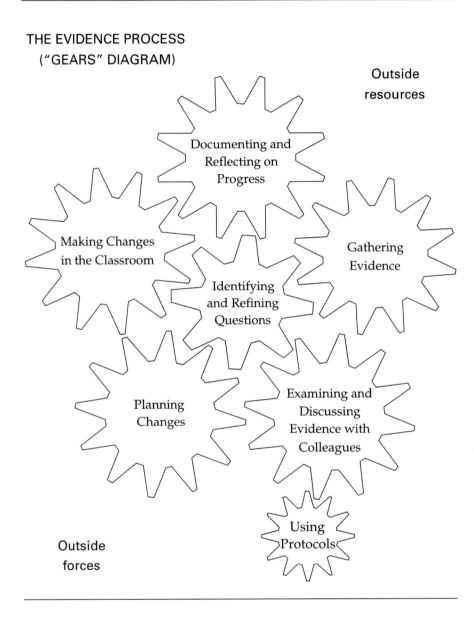

different perspectives, rather than either dismissing students' work or a colleague's as not worth talking about or simply giving each other verbal pats on the back (though commendation is often a valid part of what happens in protocols).

In groups of colleagues, there are always emotional issues of status and identity at play. Protocols help to structure the interaction so these issues don't derail the inquiry. They can also help to level the playing field to facilitate conversation among veteran teachers, "expert" teachers, and new teachers. When groups focus on questions of equity, which often surface deeply personal opinions and assumptions about issues of race, gender, culture, and fairness, it is particularly important to structure the conversation (and facilitate it) so that participants will feel safe and the conversation will be open and productive.

Purposes for Protocols. Different purposes are served by different protocols (Allen, 1998; McDonald et al., 2003; Project Zero, 2001). Inquiry groups in schools exploring how well students are meeting particular learning goals or standards often use a protocol that starts with looking at what the goal is and what it calls for in student work, then looking at multiple samples of student work at different levels and considering how different students approached that benchmark or standard. This kind of conversation often contributes to teachers developing new understandings of how to support students in learning a specific skill or concept.

Alternatively, in a group focused on how different instructional approaches support student writing, it was helpful to use a protocol in which one teacher presented one or more samples of student work from the same task without providing any contextual information about the students or the task itself. This protocol allowed participants to find strengths and possibilities in the work they might have overlooked had they known the task ahead of time. Their descriptions and questions provided a foundation to discuss implications for further instruction, as well as to consider other kinds of evidence that they would like to explore in future meetings.

Looking at Other Data with Protocols. Protocols are also helpful in looking at other data. Too often data, particularly quantitative data, are used by one person, usually the principal, to tell people what they need to be doing. This rarely leads to effective changes in practice. Rather than assuming we all come away with the same impression or lesson from test data or a set of surveys, it is useful to structure the conversation so that participants can share their individual perspectives on the data, raise questions about them, and then have a discussion about how they might act in light of what they've discussed.

Protocols are particularly important when observations of classrooms or peers are involved. Let's face it: Having somebody come into your classroom and observe you or your students can be intimidating. To lower the anxiety and maximize the chances for learning from the experience, groups use protocols in a variety of ways. In one school, groups used a protocol that calls for the teacher being observed to share her goals for the lesson in advance and also identify what she would like the observer(s) to look for, typically something that relates to the teacher's or group's inquiry question. Observers keep notes during the class observation based on that initial conversation. A follow-up conversation begins with the teacher who taught the class sharing her or his impressions of what happened, followed by comments by the observers about what they saw and how it relates to what the teacher had asked them to focus on.

While using a reading or video from outside the school doesn't require the attention to safety that is necessary when looking at samples of student work or observing each other's classrooms, it is still useful to approach such research with a structure. For example, before viewing a videotape the group may talk about what kinds of things they will be looking for and how they will discuss what they've seen. For reading, it is sometimes useful to begin the conversation with a discussion question or a round of sharing sentences or brief passages that participants found provocative or puzzling.

While protocols have proven extremely valuable to many inquiry groups, it's important to note that some groups function very well without using explicit protocols for their conversations. They develop and practice their own routines and models for conversation that move inquiry forward, as seen in the inquiry groups at Melrose Elementary School described in Chapter 6. (Table 2.1: Selecting Work to Present, as well as the references in this chapter, may be useful in selecting the protocols to use. Chapters 4 and 5 consider protocols with varied purposes.)

Facilitating Inquiry

Inquiry groups are engaged in a complex, emotionally demanding undertaking. Most groups rely on a facilitator or facilitators to help them function effectively. Facilitating an inquiry group is substantially different than, for example, running a workshop or mentoring a more junior teacher. While it requires leadership, its goal is to support and allow the group members to learn from each other, through interaction and engagement with questions and data, rather than directly from the facilitator.

Various inquiry groups handle facilitation in a different manner. One of the most significant decisions to make is whether the facilitation will be handled by someone from within the school (a teacher, administrator, curriculum coordinator) or somebody from outside the school—such as a school coach provided by the district or somebody from a partner organization or institution (college or university).

The Benefits of Insiders. There are advantages to having "insiders" facilitate groups. Certainly they will know the school context and culture better than any outsider will. This solution also provides an extraordinary opportunity for teachers to hone facilitation skills. However, facilitating one's colleagues is often more challenging for insiders than it appears. Facilitation not only requires skill, which can be developed, but also requires the acceptance of the authority and responsibility to play a special role within a group of peers. Historically, teaching has not been a profession that supports this kind of leadership. A teacher who takes on a special role is, or perceives she will be, seen by her peers as somehow suspect. Fortunately, this norm of teaching is changing, if gradually, as teachers begin to play different roles within schools (for example, accepting the mantle of "lead teacher").

The Role for Outsiders. Whether or not a group has an "inside" facilitator, there continues to be valuable roles for "outside" facilitators in working with groups and schools. Outsiders are valuable because they bring skills and experience in facilitating in different settings. And, because they have an outsider's perspective, they are often able to ask questions about a group's work that would be difficult for insiders to ask or share resources that don't exist within the group. They may play an especially useful role in helping groups develop internal facilitation skills and capacities, thus "working themselves out of a job."

Combining Inside and Outside Facilitation. In some schools, facilitation is handled by a combination of insiders and outsiders. In schools participating in Project Zero's Evidence Project (Project Zero, 2001), the outside facilitator (a liaison from Project Zero) provided most of the initial facilitation. Teachers within the groups (designated as "school-based facilitators") gradually took over planning the agenda for meetings, communicating with group members, facilitating protocols during meetings, and documenting the meetings. The early modeling by the outside facilitator was useful to the school-based facilitators in learning effective strategies and developing their own facilitation repertoires. In time, other teachers within the groups began to facilitate parts of the meeting, and several went on to become the school-based facilitator for other inquiry groups.

Facilitators of inquiry groups, whether coming from the inside or outside, benefit from opportunities to discuss facilitation with other facilitators. In the project described above, regular meetings brought together school-based facilitators from multiple schools with the researchers who acted as outside facilitators. These meetings provided a valuable forum for sharing experiences, problem solving, and reflecting on the role of facilitator. (The case studies that follow this chapter provide a range of facilitation models.)

Documenting Inquiry

Another what-happens-at-the-table activity that is often overlooked is documentation. We don't usually think of documenting what happens at the family dinner table—fortunately, perhaps! However, the discussions of teacher inquiry groups offer enormous potential for professional learning. That potential can be expanded by considering how to document what happens at the meetings (and, sometimes, in between them).

Documentation can sound like an onerous task, especially to teachers who are already overloaded with stacks of paperwork. But inquiry groups have found ways to document their process without breaking their backs doing it, including:

- *Minutes*: Having the facilitator or a group member keep minutes of the meetings, noting what work was shared and by whom, what questions arose, and any particular recommendations or outcomes from the discussion.
- *Records*: Using meeting record forms, on which participants record who presented, the questions being discussed, the protocol used (if any), who facilitated, the data examined, and some highlights from the group's discussion.
- *Taking stock*: Scheduling periodic "taking stock" discussions to reflect on how the group's process is helping to address its purposes and questions. These reflections can be written down and collected, or the facilitator might take notes from the group's conversation. (It is also helpful to tape-record such conversations for possible replaying or transcription.)
- *Journals*: Keeping journals or simply taking time to do some brief reflective writing at the end of some (or all) meetings. These writings can be read aloud or shared with a partner, or just kept in a folder as an ongoing record of personal reflection.
- *Portfolios*: Keeping group or individual portfolios of materials from meetings, including copies of the groups' inquiry question(s), protocols used, samples of student work, and other data presented.

Portfolios may also contain individual and group reflections on the inquiry process and its outcomes—for example, summaries of journals or notes from "taking stock" discussions.

- *Taping*: Audio- or videotaping a portion of a regular group meeting to spur reflection on a group's process and progress. It may be helpful to have an outside partner come in to make the tape and, perhaps, facilitate the reflective conversation that employs it.

Teachers and groups tend to see the value of documentation when it is actually used to feed the work. This is easier said than done, given the multitude of responsibilities that teachers face and the amount of time generally dedicated to inquiry. Using documentation can be as simple as the facilitator referring to notes from a previous meeting and asking the group, "Did we do what we said we would?" (It may be that the group did something entirely different, which turned out to be productive, but developing and invoking a group "memory" can help the group appreciate what it has done and with what results.)

Documentation can itself become data for inquiry, as Elena's e-mails to her inquiry partner illustrate in Chapter 3. And documentation can also provide the raw materials to shape presentations about the inquiry to others in the school community (as described in Chapter 6) and, sometimes, outside it—such as at a conference or in a workshop.

How Is the Table Supported?

Inquiry is rarely, if ever, built into a teacher's or school's professional life. Because it is, therefore, added to an already full (or overfilled) schedule and structure, careful planning and continual support are needed to get it going and to sustain it. Some of that support is very visible, carried out in faculty meetings and strategic planning meetings, while much is out of view, carried out in one-on-one conversations or in making up a professional development schedule for the month.

School and district administrators play an enormously important role in planning and supporting inquiry. They are involved in framing the purposes for inquiry and making decisions—including those discussed above—about who will participate in groups and who will facilitate, to name just a few. While the ways in which these decisions are made will naturally vary from one school to another, principals in schools that commit to an inquiry approach typically involve representatives from the school community, especially the faculty, in making decisions.

One elementary school, for example, formed a leadership team that included administrators, teachers from all levels, and curriculum coordinators to work with outside consultants to create a plan for its study groups.

This team continued to meet monthly during the first year of the study groups to consider how best to support their work. The middle school described in Chapter 5 convened representatives from the faculty, as well as from the school's partner organization, at key points in the evolution of its inquiry process.

Time for Inquiry

Principals and other administrators support inquiry in many ways. Probably the single most important way, both practically and symbolically, is their provision of time for inquiry groups to meet. To be effective, collaborative inquiry requires a significant commitment of time on the part of the participants. There is no formula for determining how much time is the correct amount, but a few criteria may help:

- Inquiry conversations are complex, seek to actively include all participants, and strive to go below the surface of the questions and issues discussed. For this reason, individual meetings may require at least an hour for participants to feel they are getting somewhere and will benefit from longer periods (1½ to 2 hours).
- Learning in individual meetings is cumulative and builds on prior meetings. Meeting once a month or more frequently will support the ongoing learning and deepening understanding of participants in the group.

Carving out the kind of time suggested by the above criteria is never easy. How it is done will depend on the culture and organization of the individual school and, sometimes, the district. In some schools, asking interested teachers to meet after school hours will work, but, in most schools, involving significant numbers of teachers and sustaining their inquiry will require identifying time during the teachers' (compensated) professional day.

Some Organizational Possibilities. In arranging time for inquiry groups to meet, administrators have been creative in using time slots already allotted for professional development and creating "new" blocks of time. For example, in one elementary school, the principal used a combination of district staff development dollars and a small grant to pay for substitutes to release teachers to participate. Rather than having shorter, more frequent meetings, these groups were able to meet for a half day once a month. This provided time to go into their work in depth while still maintaining enough continuity to sustain the momentum.

Here are some other possibilities: Middle schools often designate common planning time for interdisciplinary teams to meet while students are in noncore classes. This arrangement presents a trade-off: while it frees up core teachers for inquiry, it isolates the noncore teachers. To avoid this problem, a number of New York City alternative high schools have taken advantage of the time periods when students are involved in weekly half-day internships for inquiry groups to meet.

Staff meetings offer possibilities for inquiry as well. However, it is easy for the inquiry part of the meeting to get squeezed out by more pressing concerns or the special interests of one or more of those present. Administrators have recognized the need to "protect" time for inquiry, holding the school and themselves to the commitment they've made to give this work the required time, even if it means figuring out alternatives for dealing with other issues (for example, using a weekly memo rather than meeting time to inform staff of important announcements). Department or grade-level team meetings have also been used for collaborative inquiry. Again, an explicit effort to identify and protect time for inquiry within the overall meeting is essential.

Scheduled in-service professional development days often provide good-sized blocks of time to dedicate to inquiry. But relying on these infrequent occasions alone may prove almost counterproductive, by whetting teachers' appetite for inquiry but not providing a practical plan for how they will get to practice it in regular, ongoing group meetings. Some schools have supported inquiry by using these in-service days for group meetings and also scheduling more frequent, if briefer, meetings.

Other Costs. In schools, as in other institutions, time is money. The costs of creating time for inquiry may take the form of stipends for participants or paying substitutes to provide teachers release time to meet. Other costs that a school may incur include paying a consultant to facilitate meetings or provide facilitator training; purchasing materials and equipment (books, audio or video cameras and tapes, photocopying, etc.); covering conference fees for teachers; and allocating funds for snacks and drinks.

Partnerships to Build Capacity for Inquiry

The support of the principal and other administrators is foundational to inquiry. Even with that support, schools often benefit from partnerships with individuals or organizations from outside the school to bolster their capacity for inquiry. These outside partners might come from the district, a local university or education school, or a nonprofit educational organization. Many districts and school improvement projects have adopted the strategy of "coaching"—that is, pairing an experienced educator with a school to work on specific projects with mutually understood goals.

Coaches have been effective in helping schools develop their capacity for inquiry. Some of the ways in which coaches, and other outside partners, support inquiry are:

- Working with the administration and faculty representatives in planning for inquiry and on how to sustain and expand inquiry within the school
- Facilitating inquiry groups and working with teachers to develop facilitation skills
- Convening and facilitating meetings of inquiry groups from multiple sites
- Documenting a group's learning and process (and reporting back to the group).

Some of these roles appear as part of the case studies that follow. For example, "Network Day" meetings or "Reviews" convened by outside partners bring together inquiry group participants from several schools and play a role in supporting and deepening individual sites' inquiry processes, as described in Chapters 3 and 4.

While the outside partner or coach may play an ongoing role within the school, the goal should not be for the outsider to lead the inquiry process but rather to help the insiders develop the capacity to lead their own. In forming effective partnerships, it is important that both "parties" share an understanding of the purposes for inquiry identified by the school and by groups. Schools and partner organizations may have different priorities or time lines, which, if not aired and discussed, may weaken chances for effective inquiry.

Other Supports for Inquiry

Providing time for inquiry and involving outside partners are just two ways that administrators support inquiry. They also support it through consistently validating inquiry as a significant, important, and ongoing part of the school's work. Leaders do this in a number of ways, some of which are discussed below.

Offering Incentives for Participation. Incentives take many forms: releasing teachers from classroom responsibilities to participate in groups; arranging for teachers to receive professional development points or continuing education units; supporting teachers in attending or making presentations at conferences; and so on. For example, in one school, the principal was able to arrange with a local university for teachers who participated in the groups to receive graduate credit for a course in teacher research, based on participation in inquiry group meetings, additional readings, and writing a paper about their inquiry.

Communicating, Promoting, and Advocating. As we've seen, inquiry takes time to develop. In a school's or district's rush for results, the work of the inquiry groups may be vulnerable to being scaled back or cut entirely to make room for another initiative. Principals committed to inquiry find ways to publicly endorse its value within the school community and within the district's political context. This can be as simple as taking time at a faculty meeting to talk about how the work is beneficial to the school or inviting visitors from other schools in the district to observe a group meeting and to talk with the inquiry group participants about their work afterwards. In one school, the principal asked teachers from an initial inquiry group to plan a presentation about their work for the whole faculty, which led to the creation of additional groups.

Making Necessary Adjustments. It is important to give inquiry groups time to develop in order for participants to learn about each other, their purposes and questions, and the tools of inquiry. However, it is equally important to regularly take stock of what's happening in the groups and, where appropriate, make changes. The most natural time to do this is at the end of an inquiry group's year. This kind of taking stock often happens through a combination of reflective conversations within the groups and meetings with the principal and other administrators. However, there are times when administrators and groups can't wait until the end of the year to think about adjustments. In monitoring the inquiry process and listening to participants, a principal may judge that a more immediate reconsideration of purposes or organization of the process is necessary, as related in Chapter 5. (The "table" of decisions we have described in this chapter may provide a helpful tool for thinking about how the work might be adjusted as the group is revisiting its purposes.)

Considering Expansion and Growth. This may be one of the most enjoyable aspects of a principal's support for inquiry, but is no less important or challenging. When results of early stages of inquiry justify expanding the work, administrators are faced with a range of important decisions. Given the significant teacher turnover that many schools experience, administrators need to think carefully about how to maintain and renew groups that already exist. This may include creating a process for bringing new teachers into existing groups or reconfiguring groups to create a balance of both experienced and new participants.

In reconfiguring existing groups, it is important to recognize that group participants tend to develop trust and comfort in working with one another over time and may resist separating or taking on new members. However, there is often value in bringing new participants into existing groups, allowing the new members to benefit from the group's experience with inquiry and allowing the "veteran" members to benefit from the fresh perspectives that newcomers bring. In one school, participants in an inquiry group that had worked together for several years became facilitators of newly formed groups, thus recognizing as well as distributing the expertise of the veterans.

Each school engaging in inquiry must consider the range of decisions presented here, and others that emerge, in light of its own context, culture, and purpose(s) for inquiry. In the next part, we offer four case studies as more extended examples of how educators in different schools and districts have come to the inquiry table. Though supporting this "inquiry table" over time posed serious challenges to all of these schools, that table also nourished the schools in important ways. Their efforts offer lessons for those who want to set such tables for their own colleagues in their own schools.

Part II

An Inquiry Casebook

The following four chapters describe collaborative inquiry projects at four different schools over the course of 3 to 4 years. The chief authors of these chapters served as either outside facilitators or in-school support providers for the individual inquiry cases discussed. These particular cases have been chosen because they represent significant variability in the ways in which inquiry was first introduced at a school as a central form of professional development. Focusing on this variety of entry points provides a wide range of experiences from which to draw for those who wish to launch collaborative inquiry work in their own schools. Along with the variety of entry points, each of these cases depicts important milestones in the development of collaborative inquiry, milestones that may help us more deeply understand both how to design collaborative inquiry and how to recognize its effectiveness.

Chapter 3 describes the recently founded ASCEND, a kindergarten through eighth-grade school in Oakland, California, where the principal believes that inquiry is central to the work of teaching, and where the faculty considered the idea of engaging in formal inquiry from the earliest days of the school's existence. The demands of getting the school off the ground, however, forced inquiry to a back burner for the faculty as a whole until the informal inquiry of an individual teacher and the results she saw with students rekindled the entire staff's desire to get involved.

Chapter 4 draws on the experiences of teachers in Maxson Middle School in Plainfield, New Jersey, where the school district and an outside support provider took the initiative to launch a program of collaborative inquiry, Reviewing Student Work, at the school. The work took root most effectively in one small "school of choice" within the larger school.

At the Harbor School in Boston, Massachusetts, serving grades six through eight, which is described in Chapter 5, the founding principal brought collaborative inquiry to the school from its inception and encouraged the practice to continue as the school's faculty grew from 8 to 34 over 4 years.

At Melrose Elementary in Oakland, California, described in Chapter 6, collaborative inquiry had been established across the whole school for

8 years by the time we pick up the story to trace how one inquiry group applied their considerable inquiry experience to new district mandates and to addressing the needs of particular student groups within the school.

As you'll see, these are not "textbook" cases. They are messy. Teachers latch onto a set of questions with enthusiasm, only to find a few months later that something more important has arisen. Facilitators and group members arrive at decisions about group configurations and the scheduling of meetings and later find that personnel or schedules have shifted. Data collected doesn't always respond to the questions being asked. And stated purposes for engaging in inquiry do not always match with the actual outcomes of the process.

Some of this "two steps forward, one step back" movement is part of the inherent, necessary unpredictability of inquiry. A method of learning that depends on discovery, inquiry inevitably presents curves in the road. These curves, however, are an essential, and often positive, part of the process, and they can lead to deeper discoveries, new ideas, and more learning.

These cases, however, also reveal other, less productive kinds of obstacles. Time for group meetings is usurped. Collaborative inquiry is given second place to a new district initiative. Staff are moved without consideration of their roles in a collaborative team. Such obstacles grow out of the fragility of the conviction—especially among higher-level policy-makers—that collaborative teacher inquiry is an essential ingredient of creating a powerful learning community for students. For policymakers and school people who do believe in collaborative inquiry, the practice is hard to maintain in the face of all of the other urgencies in the lives of schools, students, and individual teachers. In the current policy environment, which does not typically provide designated time for teacher inquiry, supporting this practice on the school level over the long term requires a constant balancing act, as other needs compete for attention.

And yet we would argue that even now—or especially now—it is a balance worth seeking. Aside from the complications evident throughout the following chapters, there is something that makes the schools described in these cases different from schools where collaborative teacher inquiry has not yet been tried. Part of it is a function of collaboration itself. The teachers in these schools are talking about their teaching with each other. They've broken the silence, opened the closed doors. These schools, in which adults have built powerful professional relationships, feel warmer, more open, more cohesive. And it goes a step beyond collaboration. These teachers are not only collaborating, but they are collaborating in developing an "inquiry stance" toward their work—a stance that helps them make sense of the other policy initiatives and

Table II.1. Starting Points for Cases of Collaborative Inquiry

Name of School	Stated purpose for inquiry	Who is at the table?	What is on the table?	What happens at the table?	What supports the table?
ASCEND	A teacher questions state standards and chooses to research what he or she sees as a missing standard—learning to like reading	At first: An individual teacher, engaging in active e-mail exchange with coach from outside organization. Later: Whole faculty, in inquiry groups.	Teacher journals and e-mail letters Student surveys Student assignments and reading logs	Teacher learns the skills of teacher inquiry and introduces them to his or her colleagues	Teacher penchant for writing reflective e-mails Coach/mentor from support organization Active principal support
Maxson	Purpose stated by district: to improve instruction through the regular review of student work	Mixed grade-level teams of teachers led by internal facilitator. Also periodic cross-school meetings.	Student written work Videotapes of students explaining their work	Group uses protocol to guide discussion of student work brought by individual teachers; internal facilitator. Protocol focuses on strengths, not deficits, of student work.	Teachers have 45 minutes every 2 weeks for review of student work Support from outside organization Release time for cross-school reviews Active principal support

Table II.1. (*continued*)

Name of School	Stated purpose for inquiry	Who is at the table?	What is on the table?	What happens at the table?	What supports the table?
Harbor	Purpose formulated by the whole faculty over time: to develop a shared sense of expectations and criteria for high-quality "learning expeditions."	Subject-matter groups alternating with whole faculty group (up to the full 34 staff involved). Facilitation initially by liaison from partner organization; later, by teachers in the groups.	Student work in specific subject areas, including single pieces of work; progressive drafts; whole class sets. Teacher work, including lesson plans, rubrics, etc.	Group uses protocol to guide discussion of work brought by individual teachers Conversations framed by a "cycle of inquiry."	In the first 2 years: Twice-a-month meetings of 1.5 hours during regularly scheduled faculty meetings. Later: Once-a-month meetings of 1.5 hours during standard early release day. Support from outside organization Active principal support
Melrose Elementary	Team purpose: To reflect on how to meet the language development needs of African American and Southeast Asian students in primarily Latino school	Cross-program and cross-grade-level teams of teachers.	Student data Teacher-produced curriculum Student work Research and articles External curriculum Parent interviews	Loosely structured dialogue Sharing of classroom practice Discussion of school-wide issues Conversations framed by a model of a "cycle of inquiry"	Two hours allocated once a month on early release days Facilitation/coaching by outside organization Mid- and end-of-year sharing with whole faculty Active principal support

reforms that sweep through the school, helps them broach controversial issues, and palpably improves their teaching.

These cases are meant to provide a visceral sense of what it is like to collaborate and to develop an inquiry stance. They also provide evidence to support one of the central claims of this book: that teachers who are actively engaged in inquiry and discovery are ultimately more capable of nurturing students' abilities to inquire and discover.

To provide more of a context for the cases, we map them in broad strokes in Table II.1, according to the categories that were introduced in Chapter 2. Then, following each case, we provide commentary and note questions. Following all the cases, we bring together several of the themes noted along the way in a brief cross-case analysis.

Chapter 3

Beginning with One Teacher: Inquiry at ASCEND

ELIZABETH RADIN SIMONS

How does an outside support agency introduce teacher inquiry to a school staff? The Teacher Inquiry Project (TIP) of the Bay Area Coalition for Equitable Schools (BayCES) had established teacher inquiry teams in five schools in the BayCES network. TIP had entered these schools by contacting the school administration and leadership teams with which they co-constructed the inquiry work. In the fall of 2001, BayCES tried a different route of entry into a school, a more "bottom-up" approach at ASCEND, a new small public school in Oakland, California. Inquiry began informally at ASCEND when a BayCES coach developed a relationship with a teacher at the school and introduced her to teacher inquiry. After the teacher had some experience looking at her practice through inquiry and became convinced of its great value, she brought the idea to her colleagues. They listened and took her advice, and the staff decided to experiment with teacher inquiry. BayCES was then available to provide coaching support. This second approach does not replace the earlier one, but simply offers an alternative model. There are several possible variations of this approach, but its chief characteristics are its informal beginnings, both in its mode of entry into the school and in the initial teacher inquiry. As the inquiry develops and is introduced to the staff by a colleague or colleagues, the inquiry process becomes more formal and institutionalized.

This chapter, which describes the introduction of inquiry at ASCEND, is also a case study of the first year of one teacher's inquiry. The case study illustrates a fundamental argument for teacher inquiry as professional development—the power of a teacher learning to ask questions in a specific context with the ability to follow through by answering them for herself and changing her practice. The case study also illustrates, as the teacher points out, that teacher inquiry has the potential to lighten, not increase, the workload.

Background: BayCES and the ASCEND School

Created in 1991, BayCES's mission is to create and sustain a network of high-achieving and equitable small schools.[1] BayCES fulfills that mission by recruiting, developing, and supporting school and community leaders through on-site coaching, professional development, incubation of new schools, and fostering networking among BayCES schools. The work is centered in Oakland, California, where BayCES has helped launch new small schools in collaboration with the Oakland Unified School District and Oakland Community Organizations, a powerful grassroots organization involving over 40 churches and schools. BayCES also works with schools in San Francisco, Berkeley, and Emeryville.

Inquiry is central to BayCES's work and is used as a powerful approach to surfacing inequities in the classroom and the school. Historically, BayCES has focused on whole-school data-based approaches to inquiry. However, in the last few years, it has also begun to build the capacity of teachers and teams to engage in rigorous inquiry focused on changing classroom practice and improving student learning, which, in turn, help drive whole-school work.

BayCES's inquiry work began with the Teacher Inquiry Project (TIP), a 2-year project funded by the Walter and Elise Haas Fund. (When the grant ended, BayCES built on TIP by creating the Inquiry Leadership Network.) In TIP, the BayCES coaches worked with teams of teachers from five schools to foster teachers' capacity to do effective equity-centered inquiry—developing questions, gathering data, trying new strategies, reflecting on and learning from the results, and "going public" within their own schools and with teachers from other schools and districts in the TIP Network. The goal was to deepen teachers' inquiry into their work and broaden inquiry practice across the whole faculty, with the result that classroom-level inquiry becomes a more powerful engine for whole-school change. By design, the Teacher Inquiry Project in each school varied. In particular, the model's flexibility allowed for differences in the school's history of inquiry work, as well as its internal structure and professional culture. Equity of opportunity and outcomes for students is a basic tenet of the BayCES mission. In TIP, teachers were encouraged to look at all steps of their inquiry work, starting with the focus for their question and following through to their findings, using the lens of equity. Such an equity focus is both implicit and explicit in this case study and that of Melrose Elementary in Chapter 6.

Although TIP had a full complement of schools, the project wanted to begin to lay the groundwork for inquiry in one of the nine new small schools in the BayCES network. ASCEND, an acronym for A School Cultivating

Excellence, Nurturing Diversity, a K–8 school, was a good candidate. ASCEND opened with 9 teachers and 171 students in kindergarten and grades 2, 4, and 6. Located in Oakland's diverse Fruitvale neighborhood, the school's demographics are Latino 63%, Asian 20%, and African American 16%. The school has a large immigrant population, with 64% of its students designated English Language Learners or Limited English Proficient.

The school's mission is to graduate literate students who are comfortable with the written and spoken word, as well as with technology, contemporary culture, history, media, mathematics, science, the arts, and the environment. ASCEND opened with four major partnerships: BayCES, Expeditionary Learning/Outward Bound (ELOB), the local Arts Learning Collaborative, and Oakland Community Organizations. Expeditionary Learning works with schools to develop rigorous and multidisciplinary project-based curriculum (learning "expeditions"). The Arts Learning Collaborative in Oakland is a partnership that brings practicing artist-educators into schools to work with teachers to develop art-integrated curriculum. Oakland Community Organizations is the influential congregation-based community organizing group that helped launch the new small schools movement in Oakland and institutionalize the role of parents in these schools.

Originally named the School for Inquiry, the ASCEND design team had designated inquiry as the foundation for teacher professional development and chosen Japanese Lesson Study (JLS) as its inquiry model. However, soon after, the staff decided (for many reasons, not the least of which was the challenge of getting a new school up and running) to put their original plan to use this approach on hold and devote the 4 hours a month spent on JLS focusing on other needs.

YEAR 1—ONE TEACHER'S INQUIRY

This section describes the first year of Elena Aguilar's inquiry work: getting a focus and developing a question; noticing changes and developing new teaching strategies; and meeting with other teacher inquirers and sharing her experiences with the ASCEND staff.

Getting a Focus, Developing a Question

Elena, who had been hired to teach sixth-grade humanities and social studies at ASCEND, met Liz Simons, cocoordinator of TIP, at the BayCES New Small Autonomous School Summer Institute. They discussed Elena's social studies curriculum and literacy program, as well as her concerns about teaching reading and writing to sixth graders. When Elena joined ASCEND, she was just beginning her sixth year of teaching. She had been a third-grade teacher and left teaching to get a doctorate in cultural anthropology at the University of California, Berkeley. At the university she felt "frustrated by the distance between [herself] as a researcher and practical application to the real world," and after 2 years returned to teaching. When Hae-Sin Kim, the principal of ASCEND, hired her, Elena welcomed the challenge of teaching two classes of sixth graders, each with about 24 students. At the same time she was nervous and fearful of being able to meet the needs of sixth graders with whom she felt a strong kinship. Many of the students were low achievers, and Elena was worried about her ability to bring them up to grade level and beyond. She also felt that as the school's sole Latina teacher and someone new to teaching grade 6, she, along with her students, was under scrutiny.

At the beginning of the school year, Elena and Liz talked again, and Elena mentioned that she had some questions about her literacy curriculum. Liz, who also works for the National Writing Project, offered to talk with her about her writing program. Their work together began informally and not as an inquiry: Liz was coaching Elena on her literacy program, visiting her classes, and suggesting books and articles about teaching writing; there was no inquiry-based theory of action. Elena is a prodigious e-mailer (most quotations cited in this case study are from e-mails); she has an on-line computer in her classroom and regularly e-mailed Liz with questions about her literacy curriculum. They also met face-to-face roughly once a month.

Sometime in the fall, their discussion shifted from writing to reading. Elena had been working to align her curriculum with the California state standards and was alarmed that the standards did not include students' attitudes toward reading or, in her words, "cultivating a love of reading." Since childhood, Elena had loved to read for private solace, adventure, and escape, as well as for knowledge. From personal and teaching experience, she had developed a hypothesis about reading: skills are critical but of little value if not accompanied by a love of learning and reading. She was angry about what she saw as a missing standard. Liz listened and encouraged Elena to change the focus of their work to incorporate inquiry.

Elena, like all good teachers, especially those in small startup schools, had a monumental amount of work and was regularly in danger of burning out. Liz recognized that Elena's passion about reading would be essential to sustain inquiry in the first year of a new school and in the midst of all her other pressing concerns. The shift to inquiry began very informally. Liz encouraged Elena to e-mail her anything she noticed about her students' reading. At first her reports were laconic; Liz responded asking for more detail and encouraging her to write a more detailed description.

Elena was despondent about students' attitudes toward reading; most did not like reading and certainly did not see it as something to turn to for entertainment: "They are bored all weekend (especially long weekends)," Elena wrote in early December, "and don't see reading as something that would alleviate that misery . . . kids think reading is BORING and can't understand why anyone would do it except when it's assigned." However, around the same time she reported a change in students' attitude toward writing: "They are getting more excited about writing." In mid-December, Elena shaped her first inquiry question: "How do I help my students to become young people who enjoy reading enough to choose it for recreation or a pleasurable way to spend time?"

In her e-mail observations and reflections, Elena focused on what the students were doing and saying, which is an excellent beginning to inquiry. However, Elena was not writing about her teaching. Noticing the multiple ways in which Elena was modeling her love of reading, Liz suggested that Elena record her thoughts about teaching reading and describe her practice. In mid-December, Elena wrote a long e-mail listing the ways that she was modeling how to be a reader.

> I introduced the shelves, which contain my teaching and history books, in the beginning of the year. I said they could read them as long as they put them back where they found them and don't take them home. Only Huber (the future archaeologist) read any. . . . I began talking to students about how I choose books to read that I rarely just grab one off the shelves and read it based on what it says on the back. I told them about the two people whose recommendations I always like (one being my grandmother, who reads voraciously and is usually reading four books at a time). I told them about the book club I belong to, about reading book reviews in newspapers and magazines, and about reading book reviews in bookstores. I gave them specific details about how I ask for book recommendations, what criteria I look for, etc.

Elena taught her students to write book reviews and display them. She joined in the activity, writing reviews and leaving new books for students. She also taught them to keep a log of books they had read and to rate them on a scale of 1 to 10. And, of course, she modeled this process: "I am also keeping my reading log in a public place so they can see what I read (they were impressed with what I'd read this fall—which was the time line for what they were recording). We also talked about when/why to abandon books (how long you should give a book a chance before abandoning it.)"

As she began to know her students better, Elena was strategic about bringing books that would interest them, books that not only related to their lives but also to the curriculum. In January they were studying primates:

> Before [winter] break, I mentioned to my students something about the bonobos (primates very close to us in DNA, offshoots of chimps) . . . We were talking about myths/inaccuracies in history and science . . . about how we may have come from bonobos, who are very peaceful creatures, unlike chimps, who don't fight over territory, and (this is the part the little boys loved) have sex all the time, for pleasure as opposed to procreation. . . . They masturbate whenever they're stressed or angry, they have sex all the time— males with males, females with females . . . [When the book on the bonobos arrived,] the boys, whose skill and interest I'd assessed as being very low, pleaded and begged to let them borrow it, to read it during silent reading. There had been nothing before this that they had really expressed an interest in reading.

While tracking changes in student attitudes toward reading (using multiple measures, including student surveys and her own observations), Elena had one of those "Aha!" moments of teacher inquiry, one that supported her hypothesis about reading but nevertheless came as a surprise. In January she made a chart of her assessment of students' attitudes toward reading: "I've tried to make a list of students and interest in reading, from high to low. . . . Some are easy to place at one end or the other. Then there are a bunch who I either don't know, or they fall in the neutral middle or on the high end because they are 'good students who do what they're told.' It's very hard to assess how much they like reading."

Elena had given students a survey in which they self-assessed their own attitude toward reading and, looking at the results, she realized that she had confused "students who read a lot, or read fast, or have high comprehension with students who like to read. I have to be conscious that some kids who LOVE to read are low readers and usually read picture books." In short, Elena discovered, good readers often do not like to read, while some less skilled ones do.

Noticing Small Signs of Change and Introducing New Teaching Strategies

As early as January, Elena began to note small positive changes in student attitudes toward reading, but other data still confirmed a general disinterest. On the one hand, after the winter break, eight or nine students spoke with some enthusiasm about reading during vacation; but on the other hand, Elena saw no change in student enthusiasm over classroom reading. For example, she knew the students had money to buy a book from Scholastic: "The least expensive books from Scholastic are often ninety-five cents. . . . The students seem to have a couple of dollars a day quite regularly. Some work on weekends or after school; some get allowance from their parents." Elena talked to her students about the joys and benefits of owning a book—for example, you can write in it or reread it when bored. However, only 3 of her 47 students brought money for books. At the end of a sustained silent reading session, she asked if anyone had read anything interesting and had to pull responses from reluctant students. She also reported that when the 20 minutes of reading were over, students stopped exactly where they were—even if they were in the middle of a sentence or paragraph. They were still bored on the weekends and not reading.

Elena also wrote about her own "down" times: "I'm feeling unenthusiastic, tired, and a little burned out," she wrote in February. ". . . I've been sick for a couple weeks—can't seem to get over it. . . . Also just a little overwhelmed by the magnitude of what is to be done. We also had a very disturbing incident last week with one of our students . . . drained me and depressed me."

Despite these "lows," Elena's observations of her students and herself continued. She was reading the literature on metacognitive reading strategies and began to use them in her teaching, first modeling them herself. To expand their ideas of how to read, Elena introduced her students to books on tape, again using her own experience. She had begun listening to books on tape as she drove to school and decided to bring them to her classes, telling her students that they were a new experience for her and how much she enjoyed them. She bought tapes for students to check out and also discussed her book group, describing how members shared their enjoyment of books. She described being the only group member disliking the book at the last meeting; students listened carefully, learning that it was all right to have a different opinion.

Most importantly, Elena introduced literature circles. In the fall, Liz had given Elena the book *Literature Circles* by Harvey Daniels; Elena e-mailed back, "I LOVED this book!! It was so clear, easy, and quick to read, so concrete, and alleviated many of my fears around literature circles . . . I'm so excited to do them!!" However, she waited until February to introduce literature circles for a number of reasons:

> I wanted to wait till I felt really comfortable with the students, as
> far as management, and until they felt really comfortable with

each other. I did feel that by February that had happened. I was glad I'd waited that long. I also spent the fall really just trying to get them excited about learning, and to accomplish this I'd focused on the Stone Age/history, and on truth and accuracy in history. I felt comfortable and prepared to teach that; the kids were really into it. In addition, I guess I was just overwhelmed by starting teaching here and not having any real models to follow, except Daniels [the author of *Literature Circles*]. I was anxious about diving into something that could potentially cause discord. I'd tried a variety of literature circles with my old third graders, and it hadn't been very successful.

After a few weeks of preparation, the literature circles began brilliantly. The first day was one of Elena's "top ten teaching days!" and she got "choked up at how well it went." However, the circles slowly ran into trouble. While a few groups worked well, in others, students were absent, did not do the reading, read the whole book in advance and did not re-read the sections as they were discussed, or did not have the skills to sustain discussions. Elena looked for new strategies and wondered about the texts and "the lack of fast-paced actions—[the students] thought *Scorpions* slow. . . . How do I teach them to slow down—get the changes in characters, etc. Is this why this age likes horrors and thrillers?"

Typically Elena started her inquiry reflection on herself as a reader: "Again I feel like I have to teach something that I do, I know I do, but that I'm not conscious of how I do it. Or how to break it down for them." That reflection led to a related question: "How much do I tell them my reasons for reading and how much do I wait for them to discover the reasons by themselves?"

BayCES TIP Network Day: Meeting Other Teacher Inquirers

Elena had been a "solo inquirer" working with a partner from outside the school until late February when she attended a BayCES TIP network day. At network meetings teachers meet in small, cross-school groups where they use a protocol to share their inquiry approaches, questions, and data and receive feedback from fellow inquirers. For Elena the process was exhilarating: "I was surprised actually, to realize that my data really is interesting!" Elena wrote in her reflection, "I hadn't had that kind of perspective on it yet, and as I listened to others talk about it and thought about it myself, I got really excited by how interesting it is!" This reflection led Elena to think about her school more broadly and wonder, "How can I convince my staff/principal that we should explore this as professional development?"

The TIP meeting was a critical one for Elena. She left it feeling enthusiastic, with a clearer picture of teacher inquiry, images of new types of data she could collect, insights into the role of the culture of ASCEND on her research, and the idea to share her work with teachers at ASCEND. In a reflection on the day she wrote:

> I am feeling how could there be any other way to teach effectively than doing research on my *own* students? And that there's no way to do that without gathering data. I feel like I've just been let in on a big pedagogical secret. Prior to this, I'd never really heard of teachers doing research or teaching from the results of their data or inquiry. I was reminded of how important not only the teacher is (in relation to the data gathered) but also how important the place is to the research gathered. I realized that the culture that is developing in my school and on my grade level will have a deep impact on the data I gather—that it'll look *very* different from the data gathered at your average Oakland middle school. For example, at ASCEND and in the sixth grade, it is quickly and obviously becoming clear and accepted that it is cool to read and to be smart!
>
> This is only one example of the way that our developing school culture will impact the data. Along the same lines, I am realizing what a critical factor my relationship to them will have on the data I get—I've already noticed some things relating to this in the data. (The kids who are in some ways closest to me are the ones who say they like reading the most—chicken and the egg question. They are the kids who are also most comfortable and secure with me, as opposed to the needy ones who are always desperately seeking my approval).

Introducing TIP Inquiry to ASCEND Staff

"Just have to share," she e-mailed Liz the next day, "that yesterday I shared with the staff—about the TIP day and my research—and everyone was so excited! About both! Everyone will be undertaking some kind of mini-research . . . And I got so excited talking about it, realizing that it's energized me and made me feel like my work[load] is less, not more."

In mid-March, the ASCEND staff at the school began a 4-month pilot with individual classroom-based inquiry. Liz facilitated the pilot in collaboration with staff from the school's other partner organizations: the ELOB coach, Stephanie Sisk-Hilton; two Arts Collaborative coaches, Arlene

Shmaeff and Louise Music; and Linda Ponce de Leon, the BayCES coach. Each coach supported a few teachers, meeting individually with them about their inquiry. The entire staff met as a whole group four times from March through June; teachers generated questions, did some preliminary analysis, and shared their work using protocols similar to those used at the TIP network days. In June, the faculty decided to continue the inquiry work in the following year. The group led by Stephanie continued the work begun in the fall with Japanese Lesson Study, and their inquiry was informed by its guidelines.

Liz was chairing the meetings and early on made a mistake by using some of Elena's e-mails as models of observations, without contextualizing them and explaining that they were first drafts, full of tentative thoughts and contradictions—close to a stream of consciousness. Although she had asked Elena's permission in advance and believed the e-mails to be excellent models of observation and reflection, Liz failed to consider how Elena would feel when e-mails, replete with misspelled words and incomplete thoughts, were made public. Since this was early in the history of the school and the beginning of teacher inquiry, and teachers were still feeling insecure, Elena felt exposed and embarrassed. Fortunately, she e-mailed Liz about her discomfort, and Liz apologized. She continued to use Elena's work as a model but placed the e-mails in the context of the often messy nature of inquiry. Meanwhile, Elena grew comfortable sharing unedited data, and in the end, it was one of those uncomfortable but ultimately useful learning experiences.

Elena, no longer a solo inquirer, now did her inquiry in the context of the whole staff inquiry. Although she was pleased with the progress many of her students were making, she worried about students for whom reading was still "a frustrating chore" and ". . . that they're not learning enough skills to improve their reading." She was equally concerned about the skilled readers:

> Some of the other kids who rated their interest in starting literature circles low were kids who don't like sharing/talking with other kids. Generally I think these are high-skilled kids who get frustrated having to work with lower skilled kids, see little they can get from talking to them. . . . A lot of kids said they were less nervous starting the second round of literature circles and that they feel more confident, but many still expressed anxiety about being laughed at or because they might not do the homework. A small number expressed fears about not being able to do all the reading, that it was too much. These were lower-skilled kids.

YEAR 2—THE STORY CONTINUES:
INQUIRY IN ELENA'S CLASS AND THE SCHOOL AS A WHOLE

Inquiry in Elena's Class

During the next school year, inquiry continued at ASCEND, both in Elena's class and the school as a whole. In Elena's class it began with reflections on the state's standardized test scores. In August, the California State Assessment scores (the Stanford Achievement Test [SAT 9]) were made available to the district. ASCEND students improved across the board, with many students moving out of the bottom 25th quartile. Hae-Sin sent an e-mail congratulating the staff, which concluded, "OUR READING SCORES MADE THE BIGGEST GAINS. Our sixth-grade reading and language scores skyrocketed—go Elena!!" On vacation in Washington State, Elena checked her e-mail and wrote Liz, "I'm still on vacation up here in northwest Washington but just got this e-mail from Hae-Sin! I sort of feel guilty getting excited about test scores, but at the same time, it's definitely a great validation that one does not have to teach to the test to raise test scores. But I am so excited!!!!!!!!!!!!!! And I just had to share . . . Elena"

Elena turned the scores into an inquiry with the students when they returned in August. She asked them to write an answer to the question, "Why did your reading scores improve this year?" The most common answers were literature circles; Elena's love of reading; the amount of reading they did; Elena's belief in them; the choice of reading materials; and the support and "safety nets" they felt at ASCEND. Students said:

> Because we read all the time for homework and in school and in literature circles. I think literature circles had the most to do with it because we had a role and had to do it.

> Maybe it's because you [Elena] like to read a lot . . . because you forced us to read and we were scared of you.

> Because you want us to go to college.

> I did better because I enjoyed the books I read, Elena didn't pick the books we read or make us read books that weren't our type. So we had an opportunity to find out what kind of books we liked and didn't.

A critical goal for Elena is academic equity, and she regularly talks explicitly with students who listen and learn about the political and economic realities of their lives and how these factors affect their academic life. In the August reflection one student cited her talk as motivation; he wrote, "[W]hen you said that Oakland students (in the flatlands, not in the wealthier hills schools) are expected to fail in college and not get good grades in school and . . . will most likely drop out . . . that might encourage us to prove to those people . . . [that we can succeed]."

In her second year, Elena observed a continuing change in student attitudes to reading. Liz donated four boxes of books to the class; and students said, "Liz is our fairy godmother. It feels like Christmas." Now when sustained silent reading comes to an end, students do not stop midsentence but beg for more time. However, concerned about the superficial discussions in literature circles, Elena is teaching the elements of literature and literary analysis more explicitly, teaching comprehension skills more intensely, and studying the discourse in the literature circles to see if it is becoming more sophisticated. She is also giving students more difficult reading assignments and teaching them the value of not abandoning a book they do not immediately like. For example, the class read a book written at a sixth-grade reading level, which they found very challenging but stuck with it; Elena wrote, "I think they now like the challenge."

Elena will teach these students through the eighth grade, when they graduate. She credits her inquiry as instrumental in her students' growth and hopes they will continue to improve at an even faster rate this year, which they must, if they are to be competitive in high school college-track classes. She worries that they will not be ready for high school at the end of grade 8, because, while they have made impressive progress, they are far from high-achieving seventh graders. She showed her students the work of seventh graders from a local private school on an assignment that the class had done so that they could study high-level work. The class liked the challenge and made many insightful comparisons of the work. Elena's inquiry now focuses on new strategies like these to encourage the students to work harder.

The Story Continues: Faculty-wide Inquiry at ASCEND

During the second year of Elena's inquiry, ASCEND opened with a new sixth-grade class and four new teachers joined the inquiry work. Teachers began to take the lead in fostering inquiry at the school. A planning team of three teachers, including Elena, Davina Katz (a new teacher at ASCEND who had been in TIP for 2 years at her previous school), and Stephanie Sisk-Hilton (now a fifth-grade teacher at ASCEND) met once a month with Liz. They designed the year's program and assessed and adjusted it along the way. ASCEND dedicated 4 hours a month (two 2-hour meetings) to teacher inquiry. In one meeting, the staff of 12 plus Hae-Sin met as a whole group to learn new inquiry skills and share their work. In the other meetings, the staff met in three smaller inquiry groups facilitated by Louise, Stephanie, and Liz. Stephanie's group remained the same, continuing the Japanese Lesson Study inquiry while she began enriching the larger group with ideas from JLS.

Each month or so the ASCEND staff broke some new ground with its inquiry. A big step in midyear was dedicating a session to the always scary but ultimately rewarding prospect of sharing individual inquiry with the rest of their colleagues. Since the fall, most sharing and support was in the small groups, which had grown increasingly safe and supportive. At the midyear sharing session, the teachers met with colleagues from other groups, using a protocol to structure their turns. They shared their questions, inquiry process, and data; answered questions; listened to their colleagues reflect on their work; and ended the protocol with their own observations. Though many had been somewhat nervous to share their inquiry publicly with colleagues, the teachers were unanimously enthusiastic about the process afterward. As one teacher wrote in her reflections, "It was really amazing to hear about other people's inquiry, and realizing how many challenges we are finding in common—and how our classrooms are microcosms of issues that we are facing school-wide." At the end of the year, the teachers shared with each other again.

School-wide inquiry at ASCEND has not been totally smooth. Several teachers still question the value of this work, but the great majority feel that it is useful. These teachers appreciate having time dedicated to reflection (even though they sometimes resist it) and welcome the safety of the small groups where they feel increasingly comfortable about sharing challenges and failures. They also appreciate the integration of the arts program into inquiry and welcome the regular dedicated time to sharing practice. In a school where burnout looms like the devil peering over one's shoulder, Liz repeatedly emphasizes that inquiry is not added work: it can be done in the dedicated 4 hours a month, and teachers visibly relax each time this is reiterated. At each meeting, teachers write observational and/ or reflective journals, which themselves are a rich source of data for inquiry. Many choose to do more, seeing the data they collect, such as samples of student work and student surveys, not as added work but as an integral part of their teaching. Sharing and analyzing this data in protocols in the dedicated time for inquiry can produce findings valuable to themselves, their school, and other schools in the BayCES network.

BayCES, as an outside partner, has also learned from the ASCEND story. Elena and her colleagues' experience provide another model of introducing inquiry to a school, a model that evolves from the very informal to the more formal, and will prove particularly useful in new small schools in which staff members are initially overwhelmed with opening a school and keeping afloat. At each of these schools, BayCES can find an interested teacher or two who can be coached, as Elena was, to pilot inquiry in her or his class and then encouraged to bring it to the whole school. A teacher whose inquiry has made a difference in the classroom can be the best person to convince a staff that teacher inquiry is an excellent choice for professional development for others in the school—or for the entire school community.

COMMENTARY ON THE CASE

The immediate impact of inquiry on teaching. Elena did not have to wait through months of collecting and analyzing data in order for her inquiry process to inform and improve her teaching: the effects were immediate. From the start, Elena invited her students to participate in her project, polling and surveying them on their attitudes toward reading. Collecting data for her inquiry, she simultaneously helped her students adopt an "inquiry stance." And this is not unique to Elena: engaging in inquiry reminds teachers to engage students in inquiry—and creates a perfect context for helping students develop the habit of reflecting on their own work. This is one piece of the "pedagogical secret" that Elena feels so thrilled to have discovered.

A deeper sense of efficacy and hope—an antidote to "burnout." Another piece of the secret, we think, arises from the curiosity, engagement, and intellectual vitality that an inquiry stance nurtures. One can look at students who aren't interested in reading and be filled with sadness, hopelessness, or anger. Adopting an inquiry stance invites a teacher to seek connection with the students and to look at their learning challenges as fascinating and important puzzles. Connection opens the heart and mind to new possibilities, and these sorts of puzzles, if explored, can suggest strategies that will bring about real change. In grappling with the puzzles, Elena both forestalled her own potential burnout and found ways to transform her students' experience of reading. Experiences of these sort are ones that keep teachers teaching.

The interplay between personal inquiry and group inquiry. As we'll see in some of the other cases, when groups of teachers or whole-school faculties adopt inquiry together, there is sometimes tension between the interests, passions, and comfort zones of individual teachers and those of a whole group. Different teachers are drawn to different questions, to different kinds of data, to different group configurations, and to different purposes for meeting.

But it is also clear, as this case shows, that there can be very fruitful interplay between an individual teacher researcher and larger groups. Elena's inquiry began privately, mostly as an e-mail correspondence, but it was greatly invigorated by her attendance at a Teacher Inquiry Project meeting, where she heard teachers from other schools talk about their research and where she shared hers. Her work gathered even more momentum as colleagues at her school decided to join her to form a number of collaborative inquiry groups. In fact, a major milestone in this case is the transition from individual and private inquiry to collaborative, public inquiry.

Inquiry at ASCEND was launched largely through the initiative of an individual teacher—with the help of an outside coach, a supportive principal, and enthusiastic colleagues. As we shall see in the following case, inquiry can also be seeded at a school through the impetus of the school district.

NOTE

1. This description of BayCES also applies to the case study, in Chapter 6, of Melrose Elementary School, which is also a BayCES school.

Chapter 4

A District Initiates: Inquiry at Maxson Middle School

ALEXANDRA WEINBAUM AND
KARI NELSESTUEN

INTRODUCTION

Thirty teachers and administrators refilled their coffee cups and pulled chairs around a video monitor in the hotel conference room. The audience, including teachers from two districts, principals from five middle schools in those districts, and district staff, were participants at a Reviewing Student Work workshop conducted by the Academy for Educational Development (AED). The lights dimmed as a sixth grader from Maxson Middle School in Plainfield, New Jersey explained a mathematics project in data collection, graphing, and analysis to an interviewer. The video then followed one sixth-grade class as it moved through the day in four subjects—mathematics, language arts, social studies, and a computer class—each time focusing on the students as they answered questions or talked about what they were doing and why.

To the audience at this workshop, the video was a representation—an artifact—of student work. It was produced by teachers in the school and by the AED staff. During the video, members of the audience scribbled notes about what they saw and heard on screen. Later in the day, they turned their attention to the bound collection of student work from the classrooms shown in the video. In small groups, led by teachers and administrators who participated in the project for over a year, teachers would describe evidence, from the video and student work, that Maxson Middle School students were thinking critically (using analysis, synthesis, interpretation, and evaluation) and reflecting on their learning. These two learning goals (critical thinking and reflection) were chosen by Maxson staff as their lens of inquiry into student work. At the end of the 2-day workshop, the teachers from Maxson received detailed feedback in the form of a report from participants about evidence of these learning goals in the student work observed and reviewed during the workshop.

The Reviewing Student Work Project

AED's Reviewing Student Work (RSW) project based its theory of action on the pioneering School Quality Review work in New York State from 1993 to 1996 and its adaptation by AED in Michigan where it is known as School Self-Assessment (AED, 2002b; Ancess, 1996). RSW focused on developing the capacity of teachers to become more accountable for the quality of teaching and learning in a school through developing and practicing a culture of inquiry and through periodic external reviews by peers. In weeklong "external reviews," critical friends provide feedback to a school about how well it is achieving its learning goals for students. Reviews are followed by further school-based inquiry—for example, through reviewing student work and other data about student learning and through study groups focusing on issues raised by the review team.

The school reviews in the RSW project were 2-day workshops, such as the one described above, in which a group of teachers presented their work and that of their students to colleagues from other schools participating in the project. The feedback provided in written reports and questions helps to foster further discussion and inquiry among the presenting teachers (excerpts from a report are included later in the chapter).

Overview of Maxson Case Study

The case study presented in this chapter is an analysis of Maxson Middle School in Plainfield, New Jersey. It describes how the school approached reviewing student work and the roles played by teachers, district staff, principals, and AED staff (who are the authors). This school was chosen because it is a large middle school with a low-income student population. Its staff had not engaged in inquiry or reflection about student or teacher work before this project. The case illustrates the various strategies that AED, the district, and the school used to "seed inquiry" with the hope of growing it into an ongoing professional practice among its teachers. It is significant and different from other case studies in this book because Maxson is part of a district in which inquiry into student work is a priority and, as such, the project described below was district-initiated. Even so, the case highlights the many challenges, both organizational and cultural, faced when creating a culture of reflection and inquiry in a school.

The chapter follows the work of Maxson teachers in four phases. The first phase documents the initiation of inquiry groups throughout the school. The second focuses on the difficulties of continuing the work amid the adoption of a whole-school reform model. The third outlines how focusing on one school of choice renewed the inquiry process. And the final phase describes the continuation of the inquiry after the 3-year project officially ended. The chapter also illustrates how, over this period of time, teachers developed significant comfort and skill with inquiry methods, as well as a growing acceptance of publicly presenting and reviewing student work with peers. This ensured that inquiry work would continue in one form or another at Maxson.

The Maxson study also reveals how powerful inquiry can be for an individual teacher and a district administrator. The experiences of Miriam Malabanan, a teacher who joined the project in the second year, and Linnea (Linnie) Weiland, the director for curriculum and instruction in the Plainfield district who championed the work and continues to do so, illustrate this point.

The trajectory of the Maxson case is outlined as follows:

Year 1
Getting Started (4 months)
Forming Inquiry Groups and Documenting Their Experiences (6 months)

Year 2
Facing the Challenge of Continuing RSW and Implementing a Whole-School Reform (6 months)
Refocusing Inquiry within a Single School of Choice (4 months)

Year 3
Reflecting on the Report from the External Review (1 month)
Developing and Reflecting on an Interdisciplinary Unit (intermittent during rest of year)

Epilogue

YEAR 1

Getting Started

Maxson Middle School stretches across a full city block in Plainfield, New Jersey, a small town 28 miles west of New York City. Although gracious mansions line wide tree-lined streets on and near the street where the school is located, few students live in them. Over the past 2 decades, the town has undergone demographic changes reflected in a school population that was once entirely middle-class and White and is now primarily low-income African American and Latino. The school district as a whole has a free-lunch eligibility of 70%, and the district has received additional funding under state legislation to equalize educational opportunity.

Inside a well-maintained sprawling brick building, over 900 students in grades 6, 7, and 8 flood the long noisy hallways between classes. All 900 students used to travel from one end of the large school to another throughout the seven periods of a day. In the same year that RSW was introduced, Maxson created five thematically based schools of choice, each located in a separate part of the building, and students and their parents chose which smaller community to join. The creation of schools of choice allowed for more flexible scheduling, longer class periods, and closer adult-student relationships because teams of teachers stayed with the same students for 3 years. Additionally, teachers within each school of choice shared common planning time with colleagues who taught different subjects to the same students.

Introducing RSW to the District

In the fall of the year in which the schools of choice were first implemented, AED staff spoke with the district leadership about the Reviewing Student Work/Improving Student Achievement project. A meeting to discuss the potential benefits of RSW for participating teachers included the director of curriculum and instruction, Linnie Weiland; the principals of the town's two middle schools, Mark Jackson and Sandra Harrison; the superintendent, Larry Leverett; and several other district staff. At first, the idea resonated most strongly with district staff, especially Linnie, who was to be a strong supporter throughout the project's duration. In response to AED's request for proposals, she wrote, "We recognize the importance of regular and systematic review of student work. To improve the quality of instruction and student learning in our middle schools, our staff must learn to reflect about their practices and the work of their students." The district's commitment to the project was demonstrated by the appointment in each school of several teachers to serve as coaches, known as RSW facilitators. They received extra salary to participate in RSW professional development and to lead groups in their schools of choice in the review of student work.

In late fall, the two middle school principals, district staff, and the eight newly appointed RSW facilitators—one from each school of choice in the district's two middle schools—attended the first of three 2-day workshops. These workshops were ongoing throughout the 3-year project and included teachers and administrators from five middle schools in Philadelphia and Plainfield. The workshops provided time for participants to learn reviewing student work strategies and discuss the progress and challenges of their own schools in developing and sustaining inquiry groups.

The first workshops introduced the RSW rationale, concepts, and processes. This included methods for reviewing student work regularly, which participants learned through watching a group of experienced facilitators from other schools and districts model a review in a "fishbowl" setting. Those outside the fishbowl commented on and questioned the role of the facilitator and the methods for reviewing the work.

Guidelines for Reviewing Student Work

The following guidelines were central to the methods:

- The review is conducted using a "focusing learning goal" upon which the group has agreed in advance. The focusing learning goal is the "lens" through which student work is reviewed.
- Teachers bring student work, usually three samples with the assignment, representing different levels of academic achievement.
- The discussion is facilitated by someone with some training in the RSW approach.
- Discussion focuses on describing the evidence in the student work of the learning goal—what's there, rather than what is missing— and on assessing how strong or compelling the evidence is. The discussion does not focus on classroom contexts or students' backgrounds, but rather on the evidence that the team sees in the various samples presented.
- The presenting teacher listens and, at the end, comments on what she or he has gained from the review.
- Time is set aside for summing up and reflecting on how well the review itself was conducted.

Figure 4.1 provides guidelines for facilitators who lead reviewing student work groups.

In the introductory workshops, AED used samples of student work submitted by the two districts and focusing questions that were developed by the group through a consensus-building, goal-setting activity. Group members were asked to imagine that they were from one school and that the learning goals and questions reflected their school's values and priori-

Figure 4.1. Roles and procedures for facilitators

BEFORE THE REVIEW MEETING

- Plan the agenda and time frame; schedule the meeting; circulate the student work that will be reviewed. Be sure it includes samples of work from students at different levels of academic proficiency, the assignment for the work, and delete students' names.

DURING THE REVIEW MEETING

- Appoint a documenter who will take notes and complete the documentation form.

- Presenting teachers briefly describe the work at the beginning of the review and comment at the end on what they have gained from the session. They do not provide context or background on students.

- Establish group guidelines for discussion that will support an environment conducive to respectful practitioner exchange. Discuss student work review procedures, especially that the work will be reviewed in terms of school or team learning goals, that team members should cite evidence for their points, and that they should discuss what is in the work, not what is lacking.

- Keep the team focused on task and time.

STAGES OF THE REVIEW

- Begin by asking general impressions regarding how well the work addresses the school's learning goals. Each person should have an opportunity to speak. Then ask people for specific evidence in the work to illustrate their points. Put up the evidence on newsprint.

- Check with team members to be sure that their points are correctly recorded.

- Ask the group to identify common themes in the evidence they have posted. Circle the common themes.

- Ask the team members whether they find the evidence they have posted convincing. Why or why not?

- Keep the group from getting stuck. Focus on evidence and themes that people agree upon. Identify questions or issues for further discussion and note them in the documentation form. These issues can become the focus of future meetings.

- Bring the review to a close by asking each person to comment on whether or not the group stayed on task, whether or not they felt each person's voice was heard, and on the usefulness of the discussion to them.

- Set time and place for next review. Determine what follow-up tasks there are—for example, trying out something new in a classroom to test ideas that may have come up in the discussion and selecting work for the next session that might help to push the discussion further.

ties. After the second workshop, participating teachers made the following comments:

"Looking at student work is really looking at myself. This is the real benefit, but it is also scary."

"I felt defensive because the work we looked at was from kids in my learning community. I took it personally even though I wasn't the presenting teacher."

"It was hard not to go into 'red pencil' mode and just say what was right and wrong. But if you spend time with the work, you see strengths you didn't see before."

This initial period of review took 4 months.

Forming Inquiry Groups and Documenting Their Experiences

After the second workshop, the Plainfield principals, teachers, and district staff returned to their schools to begin regular reviews of student work. This second stage took 6 months, the rest of the school year.

The first order of business was to select an important learning goal for their students, using the consensus-building, goal-setting process modeled in AED's workshops, and to develop images of what they thought this goal would look like in student work. Maxson staff decided to focus their review question on whether their students were able to write effectively in different genres for various audiences.

In the first year, each of the teacher facilitators trained in the AED workshops led approximately five reviews for mixed grade-level groups in their particular school of choice during a 45-minute common planning period. The facilitators were responsible for collecting the student work, copying and distributing it before the review, and documenting the review itself using a form provided by AED.

At first, the facilitators introduced staff to the review process by bringing samples of student work from other schools and districts that had been used in the AED workshops. Most groups chose to look at their own work after the first introductory session, but not every team was comfortable with bringing their own work to the table. Some teachers feared that the review would be evaluative and possibly unfair. During the year the facilitators would learn that these fears were quite common. In meetings with AED staff as well as a workshop in which they were able to share their experiences with the Philadelphia schools, the Maxson facilitators would see that a common goal among all the schools participating in the project was the need to build trust and comfort with the inquiry process.

AED's training for teacher facilitators and administrators focused on several strategies for building group trust and cooperation in review teams. These strategies included reviewing student work from outside the team first, establishing ground rules and revisiting them whenever necessary, and encouraging teams to view student work as a source of data about the quality of learning in the school—not as a judgment about individual teachers or students. Although an unfamiliar concept at first, teachers began to understand that the reviews were not intended to evaluate them or their students, but rather to identify patterns in learning within their classrooms, teams, and the school as a whole. For example, in an end-of-the-year reflection on reviewing student work, teachers observed that sixth-grade students, on the whole, were writing more effectively than other students because they had been introduced to the writing process in elementary school, while the other grade levels had not. This had important implications for decisions about how writing would be taught at Maxson.

Reflecting on the First Year

At the end of the last review in the spring semester, Maxson teacher facilitators asked their colleagues to reflect on these questions:

1. What were your biggest concerns about reviewing student work at the start of this project?
2. What was difficult and what was easy about reviews?
3. What was surprising about the student work we reviewed?
4. What are your suggestions for next year?

Teachers wrote for 10 minutes and then shared some of their responses. One major finding was that the process of looking for what was present in the student work rather than what was missing was a challenge for many participants. Most teachers were used to looking at student work for a grade, often searching for what was "wrong" in a paper. Reviewing student work for evidence of what it did contain offered new ways of thinking about student learning. Many teachers discovered things about student work that they had not thought about previously:

"What surprised me [when I looked at student work] was that students performed differently for different teachers. I was also surprised when I discovered concepts in student work that I had [previously] thought weren't there."

Participants didn't always gain the same knowledge from reviews. For some, a review was an opportunity to learn more about the learning goal and how it related to assignments; for others it was an opportunity to learn what was happening in other classrooms and subject areas; for still others, reviews offered an opportunity to reflect on their own teaching practices and modify existing assignments. Some began to reflect on "taking the next steps" and what they would look like in individual teachers' classrooms. The focusing question for the reviews had been whether students were writing effectively in different genres for different audiences. In their responses, many teachers talked about the need to learn how to conduct writing conferences with individual students. They also made suggestions for improving the reviews. These included less interruption from outsiders, common team planning periods, and more interdisciplinary activities.

Maxson's principal, Mark Jackson, allocated common planning time for schools of choice and asked that reviews of student work be held twice a month in 45-minute periods. However, some teachers were absent, reported late, or left early due to other commitments. Perhaps this reflected concerns about both the usefulness and fairness of the process. Some teachers felt that in the future they needed to be more specific in their review sessions about how to follow up in the classroom.

YEAR 2

Facing the Challenge of Continuing RSW and Implementing Whole-School Reform

Through funding from the Comprehensive School Reform Act, the Plainfield School District began to implement America's Choice, a whole-school reform model in its elementary and middle schools. It was chosen as a reform model focusing on standards and providing professional development in standards-based instruction and assessment—a district priority. The model also contained an inquiry component, which district leaders and Mark Jackson thought would build on the work accomplished by teachers in the first year of Reviewing Student Work. RSW had laid the groundwork by encouraging teachers to collaborate in reviewing student work and by equipping them with specific strategies for identifying a learning goal. District leaders and school administrators felt that RSW and America's Choice were complementary.

At one of the first staff meetings of the school year, Mark attempted to convince staff of the benefits of implementing these two programs simultaneously. He posted several sheets of newsprint on the wall. On the left side "Reviewing Student Work" was written. On the right, "America's Choice Reform Model." The poster listed similarities between the RSW ideas the school had already piloted in the prior year and the new reform model.

When schools of choice met to review student work later that fall, they introduced the new America's Choice approach to reviewing student work, which teachers dubbed "sticky-note reviews." The reviews examined student work in relation to one of the standards from America's Choice. During these reviews, teachers used Post-its to note evidence that a student was meeting a particular subject-area standard as well as what was lacking. Teachers were expected to use the "sticky note" approach to assessing student work in team reviews and in their own classrooms (e.g., in conferences with students about their work).

It was clear to AED staff that this approach differed considerably from the one they had introduced. It used content-area standards, rather than teachers' questions as the lens through which work was viewed and also in the search for what was not in the work. This, in AED's view, left too little time for describing and understanding what students were able to do. In short, without consciously choosing to do so, Maxson had embraced another approach to inquiry that was at odds with the program that AED had already introduced at the school. As the year progressed, more and more processes and expectations from America's Choice were introduced at Maxson. Teachers were expected to learn the new standards, post them in their classrooms, and tie each lesson to those standards. Their common planning time and most staff meetings were dedicated to issues related to the new reform model. Many staff members felt overwhelmed by the fast pace of reform and struggled to understand and meet the changing expectations. The two America's Choice coaches in literacy and math, although very supportive of the approaches that AED had introduced, had little time to address them. This period of back-and-forth between the two approaches to inquiry took 6 months.

Refocusing Inquiry Within One School of Choice

Commitment to reviews of student work remained strong among some of the teacher facilitators, the principal, and the district staff, especially Linnie Weiland. This group of RSW leaders had the advantage of attending RSW workshops with staff from Philadelphia. They felt comfortable reviewing student work and discussing their experiences as RSW leaders. This group felt that, even in the face of so many changes at Maxson, inquiry into student work, as introduced by AED, had to be part of the professional culture.

In the workshops held with the Philadelphia schools, Linnie expressed her disappointment that some of the facilitators were no longer meeting with their groups and reviewing student work. She said, "If I were in your place I would be exhilarated to be able to provide this kind of leadership in my school" and wondered why several facilitators had chosen not to "step up to the plate." In their responses, a few teacher facilitators spoke of the confusing messages coming from the district and school about priorities and the many America's Choice requirements and the Reviewing Student Work inquiry groups. They felt that the burden of deciding between these priorities should fall on the administration and should not be left up to them.

In the second year of the project, the Maxson principal, Linnie Weiland, and the Maxson teacher facilitators participated in a 2-day workshop that was an external review of middle-grades student work from a small K–8 school from Philadelphia, a review similar to the one described at the beginning of this chapter. Together with teachers and administrators from both districts, they spent two intense days pouring over written and video artifacts focused on issues of teaching and learning. At the end of the review, the Maxson team listened to the Philadelphia teachers comment on their experience. One Maxson teacher stated, "I think this [a similar review in a 2-day workshop] will help all of us teachers focus on the [learning] goal and get us heading the same direction."

External Review of One School of Choice

Recognizing an opportunity for Maxson teachers to have a similar learning experience, the Maxson representatives volunteered their school for the next 2-day external review by staff from both districts. However, given the many changes at Maxson and the size of the faculty, they knew a review of the entire school was not feasible. Mark and Linnie and the teacher facilitators decided that they would present the idea of review to teachers in one school of choice. They identified a school of choice with a collegial culture and a strong and well-respected RSW facilitator, Jerome Jackson, who had led the reviews of student work in his school of choice. While the school's RSW team hoped eventually to continue reviews across the entire school, they decided that, at first, it would be most beneficial to focus on a smaller group of teachers. This period of refocusing the RSW project on one school of choice took 4 months.

The sixth-grade teachers from the school of choice, Maxson Institute of Technology (MIT), agreed to prepare for a 2-day external review. Miriam Malabanan taught language arts; Stefani Dubrow, math; Jerome Jackson, social studies; Carrie Hittel, science; and Kurt Fuance, technology. As a group, they had engaged in reviews of student work using America's

Choice "sticky note method" and had participated in AED reviews of student work the previous year.

Two teachers—Jerome and Miriam—were experienced; the rest had fewer than 2 years of teaching experience. Miriam, the language arts teacher, was only in her second year of teaching at Maxson (originally from the Philippines, she had taught there and in a parochial school in this country). She was eager for assistance with teaching strategies and open to new ideas. Her colleagues described her as a dedicated, hardworking teacher, respected by her students for her no-nonsense approach to learning and her clear expectations. These qualities led to the selection of one of her classes as a demonstration classroom for America's Choice. This involved working very closely with the literacy coach to implement America's Choice standards, structures, and routines and periodically coteach classes with the coach, while other teachers observed.

Miriam and her MIT colleagues worked intensively with staff from AED to choose a learning goal that was important to them. After several discussions about learning priorities across the curriculum, the team chose a learning goal they felt was important to all their students: "Students will demonstrate higher-order thinking skills (analysis, synthesis, evaluation, and/or interpretation) and will reflect on their work."

The team submitted samples of student work and the corresponding assignments to AED. They also had video cameras in their classrooms for a day. In the video of Miriam's class, students discuss three books by the children's author Jane Yolen, who was the focus of their first author study. Miriam guides a discussion comparing and contrasting characters in the books. Toward the end of class, students moaned in protest when the discussion was about to end because they were excited and had more comments to make about the characters. In response, Miriam continued the discussion until the end of class.

During the 2-day external review attended by about 30 teachers, administrators, and staff from both Philadelphia and Plainfield, Miriam, Stefani, Jerome, Carrie, and Kurt first presented the context for the video and student work. They then listened to each of three teams, which were led by teachers from other schools, as they discussed the video and the student work. The Maxson teachers had many fears going into the review because of the level of visibility their students' work would be receiving, but by the end of the 2 days they felt deeply validated in their efforts.

Evidence of Success

Many of the reviewers found evidence that MIT students were able to think critically about and reflect on their learning across subject areas—

something that the teachers had been focusing on in a more conscious way since selecting this learning goal.

The following observations by reviewers describe the work of students in one of Miriam's language arts classes, involved in the author study of Jane Yolen:

> "We observed students using rubrics to assess the work of other students and make evidence-based judgments about their analysis of characters. For example, one student in the video rated another group's author study a 'three' and said, 'He made some errors in the study. He could explain more about the relationship . . . All the characters, he said, had a good relationship, but he could have told more.'"

> "We also observed students comparing and contrasting characters from three children's books. They were able to analyze an aspect of the characters which they found in all of them, namely curiosity; they also analyzed the use of contrasting characters in each story, for example the lazy boy and hard-working girl."

> "Students were also able to interpret the major theme of each story. They showed independence in their thinking. Some emphasized the commonality of relationships and others the differences in each theme. Students were also able to use evidence from the text to illustrate and explain their points; for example, 'Prince Jo Jo is a plain prince who was a very thoughtful man. We say this because he knew when he got to the cottage and saw the Princess Miserella there, he knew not to kiss her because he had three more cousins who were beautiful on the outside but also ugly on the inside.'"

Questions for Reflection

Reports written by the workshop attendees also asked the Maxson Institute of Technology (MIT) team to reflect on questions that would help them to improve their instruction and student learning. These questions included the following:

- How does MIT define reflection on student work? To what extent does this include the development of students' metacognition (reflection on oneself as a learner)?
- How can teachers support all students in the use of higher-order thinking skills in formulating valid/rational opinions, defending

points of view, and synthesizing information both orally and in writing?

- How can teachers support meaningful dialogue in the classroom to develop independent thinking and student learning?
- How can MIT expand on the practice of students reviewing one another's work?
- How can MIT further develop their common understanding of the goals?
- How can they incorporate these goals into planning and the development of rubrics?

Although the questions pointed to areas that the attendees believed MIT teachers should focus on, the overwhelming experience was one of positive validation for MIT's efforts and the students' ability to demonstrate their learning. The superintendent, Larry Leverett, attended the 2-day external review and described his pride in the student work and teaching that supported it. The "high" produced by the review motivated teachers to meet together over the summer and plan. Unfortunately, as a result of other professional development priorities and the loss of two teachers from the team (Jerome and Kurt), this plan did not materialize. (Kurt Fuance left the school for another position, and the principal asked Jerome Jackson to lead another sixth-grade team, which lacked an experienced leader.)

YEAR 3

Reflecting on the Report from the External Review

By the following fall, America's Choice had become a stronger presence at Maxson: Classroom bulletin boards were filled with student work and sticky notes attached to them with teachers' comments, the principal asked teachers to submit student work and their assignments for him to review, and teachers continued to meet with America's Choice coaches to look at student work in relation to the standards. The RSW project remained focused on the MIT sixth-grade team.

AED scheduled several 3-hour follow-up meetings with the MIT sixth-grade team during the year. During the first meeting, the MIT team read and discussed the reports from the review institute. Miriam noticed that all the reports cited evidence of critical thinking from work produced in her classroom. However, the team also noticed that the team reports had found few examples of student reflection, the second part of their learning goal. The team discussed this, and agreed to pay closer attention to student reflection about their learning in the classroom.

Teachers also noticed that students had a good grasp of why they were learning certain things—they had expressed this well on a number of occasions in the videotape—but were not able to reflect on themselves as learners. They and the reviewing team noticed that very often students simply described the process they used to collect data or write a report. The few students who were able to reflect on the challenges in learning something and what had helped or hindered them stood out as unusual.

Developing and Reflecting on an Interdisciplinary Unit

The group continued to meet, although not regularly. For most of the year, their meetings were scheduled to coincide with a visit from AED staff or a research team that was studying inquiry in several schools in the project. For their final review of the year, the MIT team decided to create an interdisciplinary project across all four subjects and review the work produced in each class. Each teacher created a lesson about carnivals that he or she felt reflected both the America's Choice standards and the critical-thinking and reflection learning goal. Several weeks later, the team met to review student work that had been produced as part of this interdisciplinary unit. In Stefani's math class, students had created carnival games that incorporated concepts of probability. Derek Kehler, the new social studies teacher in the group, asked students to research the history of carnivals in various cultures and discuss their similarities and differences to carnivals in the United States. Miriam's students wrote persuasive letters to a fictitious mayor protesting the termination of the town's annual community carnival.

During the 3-hour review of the student work, each teacher shared her or his work. When Miriam's turn came, she shared three student letters and the group discussed the evidence of critical thinking in these letters. Everyone agreed there were examples of evaluation and analysis in the three student letters—indeed, that students had gone beyond the demands of the assignment to think seriously about how the mayor would consider this issue. Team members were also amazed at how well students addressed the assignment across academic levels and how independently they thought about the topic. Students took very different points of view; one student supported the mayor's decision to save money by using it for what she or he considered more worthwhile projects. One member of the group commented:

> "A nice part of what I saw in Miriam's work is that I could see the teaching. I know what she taught to get this kind of work but I

don't see robots who have responded to it. I see kids remaining individuals. There is always that fine line when you are teaching writing between overtraining and training. You want to give them the skills they need. There is definitely an element of training in there; there also has to be the part where they make the decisions."

Another member of the group commented, "I don't see students reflecting on their learning in any of these examples." In response, Miriam unrolled a long sheet of paper that had recorded student reflections from a discussion about the assignment. Students had talked about what they found difficult in the assignment, especially trying to put themselves in the shoes of their audience, the mayor. Miriam said:

> "Ever since the review institute, all of us come up with some sort of reflections [in our lessons]. This time, instead of writing reflections, the kids wanted to have group meetings and go over what they're having difficulty with. We tried to come up with a definition of reflection first."

Miriam's colleagues said they were impressed by how deeply the students were able to think about the process of doing the assignment. Carrie said, "When I see this, I can see what the kids are capable of doing." Miriam herself said she was surprised by how thoughtful the students had been. Developing students' capacity for reflection was something she had worked on since the external review. She also expressed her frustration that students were not carrying over what they learned about writing to other classes. This, she felt, was a challenge that they all needed to address by greater collaboration in how they taught writing.

EPILOGUE

Inquiry in Maxson continued during the following year, focusing primarily on a new math curriculum and also on students' writing; however, it occurred in content-area groups that met weekly, rather than in interdisciplinary teams, as before. Miriam expressed her regret that these teams were not meeting and believed that both kinds of inquiry were needed: "I get something very different from seeing what my kids are doing in other classrooms than I do talking with language arts teachers about content standards." Other staff at the school agreed that both kinds of reviews needed to happen and that the introduction of a new curriculum in mathematics, as well as the pressure of improving scores on the state writing tests, had resulted in the disciplinary focus for the moment. They hoped to return to interdisciplinary team reviews.

CHALLENGES AND LESSONS LEARNED

The Maxson case study illustrates many of the challenges and lessons learned about introducing inquiry in a school that does not have a prior culture of inquiry into, and reflection about, teaching and learning. These challenges include competing priorities, which took the form of implementing a new school reform model at the same time that teachers were trying to implement the RSW inquiry groups; insufficient direction from the principal and district about how to address the differences in the approaches between the America's Choice reform model and RSW; and making time for the review work during the school day, especially given the many competing priorities. Because of these challenges, Maxson's inquiry work was characterized by starts, stops, and detours. However, by the end of 3 years, many more teachers than at the beginning of RSW were comfortable using student work as an important source of data about the quality of learning in their team or school.

The lessons learned about seeding inquiry in a school are discussed below. These lessons include what the Maxson Middle School RSW experience illustrates about the roles of the district and school administration; the role of an on-site technical assistance organization (in this case, AED); and the impact on teachers.

The Role of the District and School Administrators

The role of the district and school administrators was important in moving the work forward. They were responsible for bringing the project to the schools, trying to understand it themselves by actively participating in professional development, and valuing it publicly. Linnie taught a graduate course in the district, which incorporated the AED approach to the review of student work, thus providing additional support for this form of inquiry. Administrators tried to be flexible in seeding the approach in different ways in the two middle schools. Nevertheless, in retrospect, Linnie agreed that she had not sufficiently understood how long it would take to build skill in and ownership of an inquiry process. She also felt that she had underestimated the role that the district and school leadership had to take in providing guidance to teachers about the purposes of the various forms of inquiry. For Linnie, the America's Choice sticky-note approach was useful for developing understanding of content standards in the various subject areas, and the AED interdisciplinary team inquiry allowed teachers to support one another in deepening their students' learning across subject areas.

AED's Role

AED's role in this project was threefold. Bolstered both by the research and previous experiences working in similar schools and districts, AED staff provided professional development in the reviewing student work process. AED also provided ongoing support to the schools, both technical and moral, supporting changes in the direction of the school's RSW work to accommodate district and school priorities. Lastly, and perhaps most important, AED brought the districts together as a professional network, which by the end of the first year had developed its own culture of camaraderie and critical friends' exchanges. The network took on a life of its own. Teachers and administrators rarely missed a meeting as participants began to support one another, push each other in positive ways (a Philadelphia school's courage in being the first to have an external review pushed Maxson to come forward), and learn from one another's failures and successes.

Impact on Teachers

The impact on individual teachers was substantial. RSW facilitators grew in their ability to lead inquiry groups and brought what they learned from participating in inquiry groups in their school and external reviews of other schools back to their classrooms. Members of the MIT team developed greater awareness about the relationship of their assignments to the kind of student work they expected. Miriam not only changed her teaching to help students understand what it meant to reflect on their learning but also began to think differently about her role in the team and her responsibility for the quality of students' writing in other subject areas.

Miriam demonstrates the impact that well-grounded inquiry can have on teachers who are open to rethinking and continuously improving their practice. The question remains, however, of how to extend this impact to a larger pool of teachers. As one Maxson teacher facilitator declared, "How do we get everyone to have the depth of reflection that Miriam demonstrates? Is it possible?"

COMMENTARY ON THE CASE

Inquiry provides a lens for examining other reforms and pedagogical initiatives. Inquiry was introduced at Maxson—as it is in any school—alongside other reforms and instructional initiatives. Before the launch of RSW, the district had adopted "learning goals" aligned with standards that had been developed by the state. When teachers began their inquiry at Maxson, thus, it seemed natural to focus on the question of how well students were meeting specific learning goals. Shaped by the previous adoption of learning goals, the inquiry work also helped prepare the school to take on a whole-school reform model, America's Choice, and was itself further shaped by the school's adoption of this program.

It is not coincidental that an inquiry initiative would respond to other concurrent reforms. Indeed, part of the promise of inquiry work is that it can help teachers reflect more deeply on the other initiatives in which they are engaged, as it did at Maxson. This point will be illustrated again in the two cases that follow, where teachers inquire into "expeditionary learning" at Harbor School (Chapter 5), and on a mandated curriculum, "Open Court," at Melrose Elementary (Chapter 6).

The challenge and impact of "going public" within the school. The Maxson case illustrates another element that plays a role in our other cases —the challenge of opening one's work to the scrutiny of colleagues. Collaborative inquiry breaks a long-held norm of teaching—that the only "audience" for teacher work is the students and a very occasional evaluator. Breaking this norm takes courage. In particular, teachers' willingness to begin sharing relatively weak examples of student work or lesson plans that "didn't work" represents a milestone in the development of any collaborative group. As the Maxson teachers passed that milestone, they also experienced some of the palpable benefits of collaboration. Together, through a willingness to look at problems, the Maxson teachers were able to reflect deeply on their individual work and make their overall instructional program more coherent across classrooms.

The power of cross-school inquiry networks. For the teachers at Maxson, it is clear that the "cross-school review" heightened the intensity of their involvement with inquiry. Preparing for the review gave impetus to the inquiry group to address the question of whether or not students were meeting the learning goals they had established and to expand their data-gathering efforts. After the review, teachers in the inquiry group experienced renewed energy, carrying the work forward to explore new issues in subsequent years, despite changes in the group composition. The centrality of the cross-school event in this case and of the BayCES network's "inquiry day" in the ASCEND case (Chapter 3) suggests that networks of teachers and schools can play a powerful role in supporting collaborative inquiry.

How much do different structures for inquiry matter? The Maxson case raises the question of whether inquiry is essentially the same in all its various guises. Do the particular structures or strategies matter much? In this case, the inquiry model promoted by AED invited teachers to choose a learning goal to focus on and emphasized teacher collaboration around student work they brought to the table. Rather than seeking to describe what was missing or deficient, teachers discussed evidence of student learning in the work. In a different vein, the inquiry model promoted by America's Choice focused on externally developed standards and invited teachers—in addition to working in review team meetings—to post student work in their classrooms, noting with sticky notes where there was evidence that a student had met a particular standard and where such evidence was lacking.

As is noted in the case, these approaches differ both in structure and in content. How much do such differences matter? Is it likely that the outcomes of these two different styles of inquiry would differ significantly? This case does not fully provide the answer to these questions. But from our perspective, and as the other cases will show, it is less crucial to find the "one best process"—and more crucial to seek a match between the inquiry processes used and the intended purposes of the inquiry. Further, whatever set of structures is used, the vitality and productivity of the work depend upon teachers' enthusiasm for the questions being pursued.

The next case highlights the importance of the question-finding phase of the inquiry process, as it explores the evolution of The Harbor School's work with teacher inquiry groups over a 3-year period, beginning during the second year of the school's existence.

Chapter 5

Tracing a Whole-School Evolution: Inquiry at The Harbor School

TINA BLYTHE

INTRODUCTION

Like many young schools, The Harbor School, a Boston "pilot" school for grades 6 to 8, struggled in its initial years just to find physical space. It spent its first year in the cramped, makeshift space of a community center. The second year, with no permanent building available, the student body growing, and the community center already filled to capacity, the school created an annex on the first floor of a housing complex about a block away. Finally, in its third year, the promise of a permanent home materialized: A building was available, but it would need to be renovated before The Harbor School could move in. Having now outgrown both the community center and the annex, the school relocated to yet another temporary site for a semester before finally moving into its permanent home.

In many ways, The Harbor School's efforts to build ongoing teacher inquiry groups mirrored its path to finding a home: Just as the school's outer structure needed to change to accommodate the growing student population, so the structures that guided their inquiry work had to change to meet the shifting needs of the school's staff. The story of The Harbor School's implementation of teacher inquiry groups is actually a series of stories, each one reflecting a particular stage in the faculty's growth—both in terms of its size as well as its experience with the tools of inquiry groups (questions, protocols, artifacts, and data to share), and its understanding of how to balance the needs of the group as a whole with the needs of individuals on the staff.

This chapter describes the evolution of The Harbor School's work with teacher inquiry groups over a 3-year period in which the school collaborated with staff from the Evidence Project, a research-and-development effort based at Harvard Project Zero. This chapter describes the strengths and the challenges of this work as it developed through various stages. First, however, we provide a further introduction of The Harbor School, the Evidence Project, and their collaboration.

The Harbor School

The Harbor School both resembles and differs from other urban middle schools. With 265 students in three grades and 34 staff members, the school is, by design, smaller than most; yet its student body reflects familiar urban demographics: 75% of the students qualify for free or reduced-cost lunch. About 65% percent are African American; 20% are Asian American; and the remainder are White and Latino.

The Harbor School's most distinguishing feature is its status as a "pilot" school—the Boston Public Schools' equivalent of a "charter school." Pilot schools are part of the school district and, therefore, subject to all the usual accountability measures, including the requirement that students perform at a certain level on the state-wide standardized tests. However, the school has more freedom than traditional schools in hiring faculty, managing the budget, and developing the curriculum. (In fact, the pilot schools were originally intended as laboratories for innovation, which then might affect the larger school system.)

The Harbor School was established as an Expeditionary Learning school. Situated in Dorchester, the school is dedicated to using Boston Harbor, surrounding institutions, and the city at large as "classrooms" in which students learn experientially. The curriculum at each grade level is organized around interdisciplinary "learning expeditions" in which students pursue extended projects and fieldwork. Teachers stay with the same students from grades 6 through 8. At midyear the school hosts an "exhibition night" in which it makes its work public for parents, the surrounding community, and other guests. At the end of the year, eighth-grade students present portfolios of their work (drawn from grades 6 to 8) to panels of outside responders, who assess the work and give the students feedback.

The Evidence Project

The Evidence Project was a research-and-development effort carried out by staff at Harvard Project Zero (an umbrella research group based at the Harvard Graduate School of Education) in collaboration with four Massachusetts public schools. The Evidence Project staff developed the initial outlines of a process for inquiry. This process involved teachers in:

- identifying questions they wanted to pursue in collaboration with colleagues;
- gathering evidence (in the form of student work and teacher work) from their classrooms to share with colleagues;
- examining and discussing this evidence with colleagues in Evidence Groups;
- developing new strategies to use in the classroom;
- collecting new evidence to share with colleagues.

(See Chapter 2, Figure 2.1: Gears Diagram.)

Although the process can be construed as a step-by-step cycle, in reality the steps did not always proceed in the stated order. For example, discussion of evidence with colleagues was as likely to lead to reformulation of the question or to gathering more evidence as it was to result in identifying new strategies and ideas to try out in the classroom.

The Evidence Project staff members shared this process with the schools. In each of the schools, Evidence Groups were formed. These typically consisted of six to ten teachers and administrators (the smallest group was 4 and the largest 24). In most schools, participation was voluntary. At The Harbor School, the initiative was a whole-school effort. Evidence Groups met regularly (usually twice a month initially, and then once a month later in the project). Meetings happened after school or were carved out of already-existing meeting time (such as faculty meetings or common planning time for teams).

One staff person from the Evidence Project was assigned as the primary liaison for each school. Similarly, each school designated one or more people to serve as "school-based facilitators" who would work with the Evidence Project staff person to guide the work of the Evidence Groups. Initially, Evidence Project staff facilitated all the meetings. Gradually, the facilitation responsibilities shifted to teachers within the groups, and the Evidence Project staff members focused on supporting the facilitators and documenting the work of the groups.

Underlying the whole process were several key assumptions about the way in which teacher inquiry leads to instructional improvement:

- The focus of the inquiry needs to embody the personal and collective interests of the members of the group.
- Student work and teacher work, if examined carefully, reveal many dimensions of the classroom culture and the learning and teaching that happen there.
- Multiple perspectives are required in order to understand the many dimensions embodied in the "evidence" from the classroom.

- Structures (such as protocols) are needed in order to foster the norms of inquiry.
- Changes in student learning depend on changes in teachers' understandings of their practice and how students learn.

The Formation of the Partnership

Scott Hartl, the founder of The Harbor School as well as its director for the first 5 years, had worked for Expeditionary Learning Outward Bound (ELOB) before starting the school. Through his work with ELOB, he had become familiar with Project Zero's explorations of using protocols to guide teachers in collaboratively assessing student work. In the first year of The Harbor School, when the new faculty (totaling six at that point) wished out loud for more time to share their students' work, they made a collective decision to devote one faculty meeting a month to that activity. Hartl invited staff at Project Zero to lead a series of five monthly meetings during the second semester of that first school year. Impressed with the school's commitment to reflective practice, the Project Zero team invited the school to participate in the Evidence Project when that grant was awarded for the following school year.

The Evolution of Inquiry in a School:
An Overview

In the ensuing 3 years, The Harbor School's work with Evidence Groups and the inquiry cycle developed through six phases. These phases were not ones that either The Harbor School or the Evidence Project staff anticipated or planned. Rather, they emerged as the work progressed and were fully identifiable only retrospectively. Each phase was characterized by one or two challenges and a meeting structure and process designed to address those challenges. Several challenges (such as finding a meaningful question to pursue as a group) needed to be revisited several times over the course of the work.

- Phase 1 (about 4 months): Finding questions and establishing group composition
- Phase 2 (about 4 months): Learning protocols for pursuing those questions
- Phase 3 (about 2 months): Adapting protocols and deepening the conversation
- Phase 4 (about 6 months): Finding questions again . . . trying to move forward . . .

- Phase 5 (about 4 months): Finding a common question and revising protocols
- Phase 6 (about 1 year): Adapting protocols and deepening the conversation

PHASE 1:
FINDING QUESTIONS AND ESTABLISHING GROUP COMPOSITION

In the first half of the first year of their collaboration with the Evidence Project, The Harbor School staff (now a group of ten) met four times, with an Evidence Project staff person serving as the facilitator. In those meetings, the group wrestled with two issues: what questions to pursue and how to divide (or not to divide) the group. At each of those meetings, a volunteer presented a piece (or pieces) of student work that the group examined with the use of a protocol. In the discussion and debriefing that closed each protocol, the faculty considered the questions that had surfaced during the examination of the student work: Did some questions seem more pressing than others? Had any patterns of issues or questions emerged over the several meetings in which student work had been presented? The group worked back and forth between discussing their focus and discussing the appropriate composition of the group, allowing conversation about one to inform the other.

The options for questions were numerous. Early on, the group decided to pursue a single question for the whole group, rather than individual questions. As Christina Patterson (at the time, the seventh-grade humanities teacher) pointed out: "As a faculty, we are pulled in a lot of different directions. Having common questions will help us to keep focused and together." However, identifying that group question proved tricky. Using the criteria provided by the Evidence Project staff, the group generated several lists of possible questions to explore. Group members weighed the questions according to several criteria, including personal importance to the group members; applicability to all or most classrooms; and closeness of the focus on student learning. Many of those questions seemed to have one of two problems: Either they were too general (for example, "How do we help all students learn?") or they weren't of equal importance for all members of the group. (See Figure 5.1, "Questions generated by Harbor School staff.")

At the fourth meeting, the group gave serious consideration to an idea that had emerged several times during the previous conversations: breaking the group into two subject matter–specific groups, one for math/science and another for humanities. The group agreed that this configuration

Figure 5.1. Questions generated by Harbor School staff through looking at student work in the first semester of Evidence Groups

- How do I connect teaching with students' personal lives?
- How do we raise scores on standardized tests?
- Will my students be ready to share?
- What kind of work can I ask my students to do?
- What's the best way to give feedback on writing?
- How do I find the time to manage and create portfolios? How do I scaffold them?
- What makes students want to learn?
- How do I increase student accountability?
- How can I manage project time?
- How do you help a community do incredibly hard work without burning out?
- How do I connect student learning with a sense of social responsibility?

SECOND MEETING
- How do we help students with very low-level basic skills engage in high-level, complex work?
- How do you help students master the structures and forms of expository writing *and* still encourage them to bring their voices and creativity to that writing?

THIRD MEETING
- How do we help students who are not well prepared to attain high standards?
- How do we get students and parents invested in the students' learning?
- How do we teach a meaningful curriculum and align it with preparing students for MCAS [the Massachusetts state-wide standardized test] and other standardized, high-stakes tests?
- How do we incorporate students' cultures within the curriculum?
- How do we help students develop the academic and social skills they need to engage in project-based learning?
- How do we respond to all students' needs?

FOURTH MEETING (THE QUESTIONS THAT BECAME
THE FOCUS FOR THE REST OF THE YEAR'S WORK)

For the humanities group:
- How do we teach students to use reading strategies in a way that improves their reading skills?
- How do we use criteria to improve student writing?

For the math/science group:
- How do we help students use problem-solving and critical thinking skills appropriately and accurately?

would solve a number of problems. First, it would give them a chance to talk in depth across the grade levels about their subject-specific curriculum and teaching—something that they had not yet had a chance to do. Second, it would allow them to focus their questions in a way that would have more immediate relevance to the concerns of their teaching. Each subject matter group would decide on a focus question for that group, rather than trying to come up with a question that every staff member would find appealing.

The group also identified two drawbacks of the plan: the loss of opportunity to talk as a whole staff about student work and learning; and the problem of how to support the work of those staff who were not teaching a core subject area (such as the special education teacher or the physical education teacher). The group decided to address the former concern by alternating subject matter group meetings with whole-group meetings. For the latter issue, they decided to talk with the teachers in question and find out whether they would be comfortable joining in with the subject matter focus of either of the two groups, or if they would rather have a focus of their own.

Ultimately, the subject matter groups were established, and each group decided on its own focus questions. For the math/science group, the question became, How do we help students to use problem-solving and critical thinking skills appropriately and accurately? The humanities group identified two questions: How do we help students to use reading strategies to improve reading comprehension? and How can criteria be used to help students write better? Of all the many interesting questions the groups considered, these questions emerged as the most urgent ones for two reasons. First, the teachers felt that developing better understandings of these questions was vital if they were to help their students tackle the state-mandated tests successfully. Second, the questions directly addressed a growing frustration for all of the faculty members. One of the humanities teachers described it like this: "We spend a lot of time teaching these strategies. And the students do know these strategies—most of them can recite what they're supposed to do when you ask them how to tackle a reading passage. But they don't do it when they read unless we tell them to. Why? And what can we do about it?"

PHASE 2:
LEARNING PROTOCOLS FOR PURSUING THOSE QUESTIONS

For the next 4 months, from December to March, the Evidence Groups at The Harbor School met regularly every 2 weeks. For most of those meetings, Evidence Project staff people served as facilitators and led the groups in using different protocols. In some meetings, every participant brought student work from his or her classroom to share in the subject matter group to which he or she belonged. In a few of the meetings, the two subject matter groups met together, with one presenter from each group presenting student work to the whole group.

While all presenters shared student work, the amount and kind of work varied from meeting to meeting. Sometimes staff shared single pieces of work; sometimes the presentation involved sharing the many parts of a multistep, months-long project. The focus of some meetings was a sustained conversation about a single page of work; at other meetings, the group browsed through 10 to 20 selections drawn from a whole class. Teacher assignments, criteria, and scoring rubrics were also offered as evidence of practice. The staff used several protocols to structure their conversations around these data. (See Figure 5.2 for a sample protocol used by the groups in examining and discussing the work presented.)

These meetings were characterized by the willing participation of the staff, enthusiastic conversations, and the continual generation of a number of thought-provoking questions, some of which related to the original questions that the groups had generated, others of which opened up other avenues of exploration. The chosen questions continued to lend some framing to the meetings; however, the work that people presented seemed less in response to those questions than to the idea that it was their "turn" to share work. While the conversations were interesting and useful for the teachers, the motivation for having the discussions seemed to become the imminent arrival of facilitators from the Evidence Project staff to lead the meetings. The meetings during this phase helped the groups to grow accustomed to sharing their students' work. The staff members were also gaining some facility with the use of protocols. But while the meetings were valued opportunities for sharing, their power as a venue for helping The Harbor School staff dig deeply and consistently into the complex issues of teaching and learning had yet to emerge.

PHASE 3:
ADAPTING PROTOCOLS AND DEEPENING THE CONVERSATION

Toward the end of the first year, as The Harbor School staff became more practiced with the protocols and developed a better sense of what the conversations could accomplish, the motivation shifted. The group members began to see the Evidence Group meetings as opportunities to address in a consistent and sustained way the issues that were arising in their classrooms on a daily basis.

Figure 5.2. Modified collaborative assessment conference protocol

Purpose: The purpose of this protocol, based on the Collaborative Assessment Conference and developed for the Evidence Project, is to help a group consider carefully selected pieces of student work in light of the particular question(s) that a teacher or group has identified.

1. Presenting teacher reminds the group of his or her question.

2. Presenting teacher puts evidence on the table (but says nothing about it).

3. Group describes the evidence (no judgment or expression of personal taste).

4. Group raises questions about the evidence.

5. Presenting teacher speaks:
   - Tells why he or she chose this particular piece of evidence to share (how he or she sees it relating to his or her question).
   - Provides some context about the evidence.
   - Picks a question raised by the group that he or she would like to discuss with the group.

6. Whole group discusses the issue(s) identified by the presenting teacher.
   - Whole group discusses what this evidence tells them about the presenting teacher's question.
   - Whole group discusses what other evidence they would find helpful in considering this question.

7. Whole group reflects on the protocol: What was it like? What did we learn?

8. Thanks to the presenting teacher!

At the end of March, the two school-based facilitators began to take the initiative in organizing the content of the Evidence Group meetings. They called Tina Blythe, the Evidence Project liaison, to let her know that the staff had set the agenda for the upcoming meeting: The faculty had decided to spend it examining evidence from the open-ended prompts in math and science that they had recently given students in preparation for the state-wide assessment every spring.

When the conversation at that meeting led to a deepening of the concern about students' ability to solve problems and think critically, the seventh-grade math and science teachers asked if they could share work at the following meeting. They had two reasons for making the request. First, they had recently attended a thinking skills workshop. Having gleaned some ideas for how to help students think critically, they wanted to try them out in their classes and have the group examine the resulting student work. Second, they wanted to share some of what they had learned in that workshop with the rest of the group. The whole group agreed to modify the protocol they had been using so that it would leave time for the additional presentation and activities led by the two presenting teachers.

For that meeting, the presenting teachers, in collaboration with the school-based facilitators, developed and wrote out the agenda and provided materials for the group. They asked the Evidence Project liaison to facilitate the protocol in which the group examined the student work; however, the remainder of the meeting (involving a combination of activities and presentations on thinking skills) was led by the presenting teachers.

Terri Grey, one of the presenting teachers, reflected at the end of that year:

> "It [the meeting] marked a kind of a turning point . . . in our Evidence Project [work]. It was a time where our meetings had been going along fine, and then my partner teacher Mark [Clark] and I had this idea to present evidence and at the same time do a presentation to the staff about critical thinking, which we went to a seminar on . . . After that time, we started thinking, 'How can we change the structure of our meetings to spend more time on teacher development and to have more ideas shared about what the work is really saying and where we can take the work next?' And from that point on, every meeting we've kind of been thinking about little adjustments we can make to be more effective in our meetings."

The groups became more conscious about the importance of building from one discussion to the next: namely, using the issues that had emerged in one meeting to plan the discussion for the next. They began to identify more specifically the kinds of student work they needed to examine and discuss at each subsequent meeting. They also gave more attention to the facilitation of the meetings and how to deploy their Evidence Project liaison strategically for parts of meetings that they felt would be best served by having the facilitation of an "outsider."

One of the additional adjustments was to include the three student teachers who had come to work at the school that semester and who were just beginning to teach classes. As one of the supervising teachers commented, "I don't think my student teacher really understands yet how much thinking and effort goes into planning and teaching. I think these meetings will help him see that."

While the whole staff agreed that it would be good if the student teachers could come to all the faculty meetings, it was the Evidence Group meetings, the faculty said, that were the most important for the teachers to start attending. As one of them said, "This is the one meeting where we really talk about teaching and learning. That's what they need to be part of." The teachers hoped that the Evidence Group meetings would give the student teachers the chance to see the complexity of teaching: that there are no easy answers to most of the serious questions that teachers have and that pursuing those questions takes time. When the student teachers presented their students' work to the faculty in the final Evidence Group meeting of the year, the faculty were able both to identify in it many instances of critical thinking and reading skills at work—and to suggest (for the student teachers as well as themselves) some specific ways of enhancing those skills.

PHASE 4:
FINDING QUESTIONS AGAIN . . . AND TRYING TO MOVE FORWARD . . .

By the school's third year—the second year of their collaboration with the Evidence Project—The Harbor School had outgrown the community center. They had finally found a permanent building, but the renovations would take a semester to complete. Unable to stay in their old space and not yet able to move into the new, the school took up temporary residence in the Dorchester headquarters of the Boston electrical workers union, which was typically available during school hours, though not in the evening.

The rooms in the union building were more spacious and better equipped than the community center's had been. But there was no storage space available. Hartl, the school director, purchased a large portable file box for each staff member, and the teachers carried everything with them to and from classes, to and from meetings, and to and from their cars every morning and every evening. With most of their supplies and materials still in boxes awaiting the move to the permanent building, many of the teachers found the task of preparing the materials for each day's class to be even more time-consuming than it had been the year before. For the nine new staff who joined The Harbor School at the beginning of that semester (including several first-year teachers), the challenges were considerable.

With the growth of the staff and the move to the temporary building, it is not surprising that in many ways, that year felt like a new start for the Evidence Group work. As had been planned the previous year, the faculty continued to meet in discipline-specific, cross-grade groups, one for humanities and one for math/science. Elective teachers were invited to decide which group to attend. The three special education teachers decided to form their own group, making a total of three Evidence Groups at The Harbor School.

The humanities and math/science groups were bigger than they had been the previous year, and the new faculty, most of whom had not had experience with inquiry groups or protocols, were not quite sure how to engage in the Evidence Group meetings or what their purpose was. In many ways, their reaction was not much different from the reaction that the teachers had had at the beginning of the previous year. But the energy that had carried the first groups through the initial ambiguities of the process was in short supply this year: The logistical challenges posed by the temporary space taxed everyone's focus and enthusiasm.

Complicating matters was the fact that the previous year's questions no longer held the same widespread appeal that they had once held. The groups again went through the process of sharing student work while they cast about for a focusing question that would seem equally compelling (or at least interesting) to all the group members.

With the bulk of the faculty's attention and energy focused elsewhere, the Evidence Project staff members again assumed the lead in the meetings. Slowly over the course of the fall, as group members shared student work via protocols, each of the three groups arrived at their questions. The math/science group began to pick up steam as they decided to concentrate on the problem of teaching reading and writing skills and strategies to students in math and science so that students would be able to explain their thinking (as was required on the state-wide standardized test).

The special education group (the smallest, with three members and a facilitator from the Evidence Project) decided to focus on the following two questions: (1) What are the special education services and supports that students and teachers can expect to receive at The Harbor School? and (2) How can we help kids to catch up and keep up? The humanities group, the largest of the three, settled on a general question: How do we create a coherent humanities/arts curriculum across the three grades at The Harbor School?

Winter break finally arrived, and with it, The Harbor School's move to its permanent site. (Amazingly, the renovations were finished on schedule.) Students and teachers came back after the New Year to a beautiful old three-story building, wood floors gleaming from the recent sanding and varnishing, a full wall of enormous, sun-filled windows in almost every classroom. The Harbor School was home.

PHASE 5: FINDING A COMMON QUESTION AND REVISING PROTOCOLS

And still the work of the inquiry groups seemed to flag—with the notable exception of the three math teachers in the math/science group, who were sharing and discussing the open-ended math prompts they assigned students on a regular basis as preparation for the state-wide standardized tests. For them, the new structure seemed to be working reasonably well. They felt that their examination and discussion of these trial prompts were giving them clearer insights into the specific difficulties that students were encountering. They also appreciated the time to share various strategies with one another for how those difficulties might be addressed at the various grade levels. For the other teachers, however, the inquiry group work didn't seem to be coalescing into the energetic, focused effort that had emerged the year before.

Evidence Project staff were puzzled: Could it be that unpacking and settling in were still commanding the staff's focus? The suspicions that it might be something more were confirmed when Scott Hartl, the school's director, called the Evidence Project liaison one afternoon in early February. He said he had received a memo from a teacher that described her own sense of futility and frustration with the Evidence Group meetings. Hartl checked with others on the faculty and received similar responses. He had called to ask if the Evidence Project staff could attend a meeting to reflect on the work and talk about what to do next.

Early the following week, Hartl convened a meeting of the school's three other administrators, three staff from the Evidence Project, and three other Harbor School faculty members who had been involved in the Evidence Project work since its inception. Hartl laid out the issues: "We're halfway through this three-year project now. When we cut back at the beginning of this year on the number of things we use our Wednesday faculty time for, we still continued to save time for the Evidence Project because we value this time—people value talking about our own work.

"However, the sense of immediacy [in the Evidence Group work] is lacking for many of the staff. There's an internal feeling for many of them that says, 'We don't have time for this.' The time is not feeling useful to them—it's feeling overintellectualized, when we have so many pressing things we need to get done."

Joe Zaremba, project coordinator at the school, concurred: "We really haven't felt the carryover from one meeting to the next this year like we did [last year]." "It just feels like the conversation stops at the end of the meeting," puzzled Terri Grey. "I'm not sure how to make that connection so that things go on."

"There are so many new staff this year," Zaremba added. "And this is the first time the eighth-grade curriculum has been taught. We're all trying to figure out what we're teaching and how we're going to teach it."

Hartl was careful to point out that while he thought the problem was serious and needed attention, he wanted to be careful to avoid a "knee-jerk reaction." He mused out loud: "What's really at a premium right now is time to spend on developing curriculum, sharing curriculum plans, and getting feedback from one another. What do we think a good curriculum project looks like? What does a good learning expedition look like? Is there some way we can make an explicit connection to that? That's the question people are asking."

As the group continued to talk, a plan emerged for refocusing the inquiry group work at The Harbor School around the question, What makes a good learning expedition? In the new plan, the staff would meet as a whole group once a month. Each grade-level team would take a turn presenting the curriculum plans for a learning expedition they were about to undertake with their students and gather feedback on how to refine it. After they had carried out the learning expedition, the same team would then bring the relevant samples of student work to share with the group so that the group could reflect on the student learning and suggest further revisions to the curriculum plans to increase their effectiveness. (Figure 5.3 contains the memo that was shared with The Harbor School faculty to explain the change in plans and how to set up for it.)

The plan was put into action 2 weeks later. To some extent, it worked to revive interest and energy in the group meetings. Because teachers at The Harbor School "loop" with their students, everyone eventually has to teach every grade level, generating a lot of built-in interest in what was being taught at each grade. The biggest drawback was the size of the group. With 24 people involved, it was difficult for everyone to have the chance to contribute to the discussion regularly. However, The Harbor School staff wanted to stay together: They felt, with so many new staff on board, that everyone needed to hear more or less the same thing in order to develop a common understanding of what makes a quality learning expedition.

A further challenge was felt more by the Evidence Project staff than by The Harbor School faculty: People were indeed eager to hear about the details of curriculum projects being planned and taught by their colleagues—but their questioning of one another tended to focus on the logistics of the planning and teaching: How long did you give the students to revise their writing? How did you set up the resources for them to use in their research? While these questions were important, especially for the beginning teachers on the staff, they tended to lead to quick exchanges of information among the teachers rather than to discussions about why a particular approach was used and how it did (or didn't) contribute to creating a good learning expedition. Deeper inquiry into the nature and characteristics of powerful learning expeditions seemed, for a time, to fall by the wayside.

The final challenge was inevitable: Not everyone had been unhappy in the previous structure—and so not everyone was enthusiastic about

Figure 5.3. Restructuring Evidence Groups: A memo from the administration and evidence project liaisons to The Harbor School Staff

To: Harbor School Staff
From:
Re: Refocusing the work of the Evidence Groups
Date: 16 February 2000

Hi, Everyone,

We have heard the feedback from some of you that says 1) there is far too much to do and 2) it would be better if the work of the Evidence Groups was linked more concretely to the urgent things that need to get done here—like, for instance, curriculum or expedition planning.

We suggest here a new focus for the Evidence Groups: a focus on sharing curriculum pieces about which you'd like to get feedback. We hope that the new focus will serve several purposes:

- It will make the Evidence Group meetings more immediately and concretely useful to people.
- It will give the staff the opportunity to share curriculum plans with one another.
- It will help us document our curriculum better, since presenting curriculum to a larger group will involve writing out the goals, steps, and time line for the curriculum piece or expedition.

To do this, we'll be using Wednesday Evidence Group time in several different ways between now and the end of the school year:

1.   PLANNING: Two hours every Wednesday for several Wednesdays from early to late March will be devoted to giving people curriculum planning time. You will be provided with both suggestions for how to structure this planning time as well as a template for outlining the curriculum piece or expedition you are developing.

2.   SHARING AND DISCUSSING CURRICULUM: Then, from the end of March through mid- or late April, we will pick several Wednesdays and devote 2 hours on each of them to sharing the curriculum piece or expedition outline with a larger group. That group might be the whole staff; for instance, if the work is focused on an expedition that everyone, sooner or later, is going to wind up teaching. Or the group might be a subset of the whole faculty (say, science and math teachers, or various members of the other two grade-level teams) if the curriculum piece or expedition is more focused on a particular subject matter.

Figure 5.3. (*continued*)

The sharing and discussion sessions will look much like Evidence Groups look now. Some teacher or group of teachers will present a piece of curriculum, and the group will use a protocol to examine the curriculum and give feedback about it. (The presenting group or teacher will also have the opportunity to name a particular question they want the group to address, such as, "How can I scaffold research in this project?"). You do NOT need to present a polished piece of curriculum at these sessions. In fact, a rough draft would be better, since the point is to give people some help in refining and improving their plans.

3. **CARRYING OUT CURRICULUM AND COLLECTING STUDENT WORK:** Depending on the timing, there may be another few Wednesdays (maybe one to three of them) where we don't have any Evidence Group meetings while people are carrying out the curriculum that they shared with the group. During this time, everyone will be teaching and keeping an eye out for pieces of student work that they want to share with colleagues.

4. **SHARING AND DISCUSSING THE STUDENT WORK:** Finally, we will have several Wednesdays from late April to late May when you will share with the group some pieces of student work that came out of the curriculum piece or expedition that you planned. This will give you and the group the opportunity to reflect on what students learned and how the curriculum piece or expedition could be improved next year.

NEXT STEPS:

As you can guess, the real trick to making this work is the scheduling, and we'll need your help to schedule the times for you to present both the curriculum and the student work in a way that is most helpful.

-   Please talk with your team members about the attached form and fill it out (as many copies as are needed, depending on how many members of your team want to work together).
-   Make sure the team leader has the completed form(s) by *Wednesday, March 1.*

Joe Z will collect them. A group of us will work on the schedule and let everyone know within the week how things have worked out.

making a change. The three math teachers had in fact felt productive in the meetings earlier in the year. While they acquiesced with grace to the new approach, it was with a sense of loss.

PHASE 6:
ADAPTING PROTOCOLS AND DEEPENING THE CONVERSATION

The next fall, The Harbor School entered its fourth year—its third year in the collaboration with the Evidence Project. The school grew to its full capacity that year: Seventeen new staff people arrived (many of whom were new or relatively new teachers), for a total of 34. Two hundred sixty-five students enrolled in the three grades.

Again, with so many new faculty, the staff faced the challenge of building a shared understanding of the inquiry work of the Evidence Groups. However, several factors worked together to maintain some sense of continuity from the previous year. First, and critically, The Harbor School for the first time was beginning the new school year in the exact same space in which it had ended the previous year. While new staff still needed to get settled in, the returning faculty were able to begin the year with at least one eye on curriculum and learning issues rather than having to concentrate entirely on logistics.

Second, the focus question of the Evidence Group work remained the same: What are the qualities of a good learning expedition? Because this was a question of urgent interest to both new and old staff, there was little of the initial hesitancy that had characterized the start of the previous year's work.

In addition, the faculty met in smaller groups, ensuring more opportunity for individuals to participate in substantive ways. At each Evidence Group meeting, the staff split into two or three smaller groups, depending on how many people wanted to present work. The membership in these groups was fluid. This made it hard to make specific connections from one conversation to the next, but it did enable the staff to see different approaches to expedition plans. And the focusing question about what makes a good learning expedition enabled some connections to be established from one conversation to the next, even if people had been in different groups in the session before.

Also at this time, the more experienced Harbor School faculty began rotating facilitation duties, and the Evidence Project staff began to participate as group members while continuing their documentation efforts.

In reviewing curriculum plans, the groups continued to draw on the protocol they had used in the previous semester (see Figure 5.4). Over the

Figure 5.4. Protocol for reflecting on learning expedition plans

---

Purpose: This protocol offers the group a way of reviewing, discussing, and giving one another feedback on curriculum plans (preferably before those plans are carried out).

1. Whole group browses through materials brought by presenting team/person.

2. Presenting team/person describes expedition plans and names a focusing question.

3. Group asks clarifying questions.

4. Group (without presenters) discusses the learning plans:
   - Group members say what they see
   - Group members name strengths
   - Group members flag issues of concern
   - Group discusses the presenters' focusing question

5. Presenter(s) respond to the group discussion:
   - What did you hear in the feedback that helps?
   - What next steps might you take?

6. Whole group reflects on the discussion and the protocol:
   - What evidence might the presenter(s) bring back to the group at a later point to show the degree to which the students achieved the learning goals?

7. Group thanks the presenter(s).

---

course of year, they began to develop a greater comfort and ease with the protocol. As Karen Engel (seventh-grade humanities teacher) reflected at the close of the year:

> "I think it's . . . gotten more comfortable for presenters and partici-
> pants over time, and when I think back to our analysis at the end of
> last year [the second year of Evidence Project work], there was a lot
> of sense of 'It feels rigid. It feels contrived' or 'The conversation
> feels forced.' For me the difference between last year and this year
> is pretty dramatic—just in terms of feeling like now the structures
> are internalized. As a presenter last year, I was like [speaking very
> rapidly and urgently], 'I want to say something! I want to say
> something! I'm burning to say something!' And . . . I [have] inter-
> nalized that, 'This isn't the time you're going to say it, so just settle

back and relax.' And the longer we've done it, the less contrived and forced it has felt and the more . . . organic."

In addition, teachers began putting a finer point on the general question of "What are the qualities of a good learning expedition?" by asking the group to focus on one or two aspects of their curriculum plans. In one Evidence Group meeting, the presenting teacher asked, "What is the role of basic skill development in a quality learning expedition?" This sparked a serious discussion of whether or not basic skills could be taught in the context of the project-based learning that characterized expeditions. The disagreement was amicable but pointed, and teachers returned to the issue in several later discussions.

The inquiry work was also influencing interactions with students in the classrooms: "It's like popcorn going off all over the building" said Scott Hartl, describing the ways in which ideas and strategies that surfaced in Evidence Group meetings were affecting classroom practice. Furthermore, the process of inquiry in Evidence Group meetings (and not just the ideas generated by that inquiry) was having an effect as well. As Joe Zaremba described,

> "I felt that these meetings helped me to think about my work, helped me to see through other people's eyes what was going on in my students' work and in my own teaching. I thought, 'Isn't that what I want the students to do, too? To be able to look at their own work and raise questions about it and get the perspectives of others and then revise it?' If the protocols could help us teachers do that, couldn't they help the students, too?"

Zaremba began having his students use the same protocol that he had been using with colleagues in the Evidence Group meetings. As the protocol required, each presenter formulated a question about his or her work that he or she wanted group members to consider as they discussed the work, and then the presenter responded to the conversation by articulating the issues or next steps he or she thought they could take to improve the work in the next phase. Zaremba reflected on the transformation of his students: "It was really exciting for them to be part of it and to reach their own conclusions about their work. I wasn't the one telling them, 'Now you need to do this, and this, and this.' They were hearing from the other students and thinking about how others viewed their work. They were really in charge of their own learning."

Toward the end of the year, teachers began to break with the tendency to bring only the highest quality work to the table. They began to share student work that had not met the standards in order to ask for feedback on both the quality and what could be done to support the struggling students. In reflecting on this growing trend, Mark Clark (seventh-grade math) hoped it would continue:

> "We need to figure out ways to be a bit more challenging to the presenting teachers and even the participants to not, you know, berate someone's work or totally discredit it but to be challenging—to ask some even harder questions about what they're doing in the classroom, how this fits into the curriculum . . . how are kids who are not necessarily the higher-end kids doing with this. Because I think that's where we need to look. I think in the last couple of protocols I've done, I've seen more of that, but that's something we need to push ourselves towards . . . to be as challenging as we would to our students, to ourselves."

Scott Hartl concurred, but also pointed out that the Evidence Group meetings had been filling a unique need in the development of the school:

> "I think it's development for us as a school, too. With seventeen new faculty this year, the question on the table was, 'What am I supposed to be doing? Help me figure out what I'm supposed to be doing.' And so having the model of strong examples of project work for this year has responded to that basic question."

In a year-end reflective conversation, several teachers noted that the inquiry groups helped teachers develop new norms of discussion as much as they helped teachers deepen their understanding of learning expeditions. As Christina Patterson (then the school curriculum development coordinator) reflected, "I definitely think there's a sense of when we think about what we're doing, we think about what's the protocol that will help us look at this better. And our learning how to structure conversations so that everyone has a chance to talk and everyone can really look at the work in a more objective fashion . . . I think that's become helpful for our culture."

The Evidence Groups had, as Joe Zaremba put it, given the faculty the dedicated time and structure to help them "learn to talk about learning."

COMMENTARY ON THE CASE

Inquiry proceeds in a nonlinear fashion. We argued in Chapter 2 that the progress of collaborative inquiry groups is neither necessarily linear nor neatly cyclical. Inquiries can lead both to anticipated outcomes and unintended, even serendipitous outcomes that can affect the shape and direction of future inquiries. In this case, there are clear examples of nonlinear aspects of this work. The Harbor teachers spent several months at the beginning of the project seeking to formulate the questions that were most likely to animate them over time—and in conjunction with that, seeking to determine the group constellations that made the most sense in view of the questions. By the following year—even before the teachers had traveled a complete "cycle of inquiry"—these questions had lost their widespread appeal, and the process of question-seeking began again.

This sort of "nonlinearity" is an inevitable feature of the collaborative inquiry process—and it does not necessarily indicate a lack of progress. Inquiry is a fundamentally responsive form of professional development. As large numbers of new staff joined the school each year, their individual needs and interests necessarily shaped the needs and interests of the school as a whole, changing the focus and structure of the work over time. A similar sort of responsiveness can be seen in Harbor's move from holding subject matter group meetings alternating with whole-group meetings, in the first year, to holding only whole-group meetings at the end of the second year, and shifting back to smaller, fluid groups in the third year of the project. As unstable as it might appear, such vacillation often represents a deepening of the work, as group members learn to match group configurations with their needs.

The principal needs to run interference to protect the inquiry work. There are other kinds of "nonlinearity," on the other hand, which are quite common—but certainly do not contribute to the goals of collaborative inquiry. In this case, the principal works to limit these kinds of curves in the road. He ensured that the time set aside for collaborative inquiry would not be eaten up by something else. As in the Maxson case (Chapter 4), where the principal sought to highlight the coherence between inquiry and the America's Choice initiative, so, too, the principal and the staff here sought to establish coherence between the inquiry work and the school's curricular focus (learning expeditions). If the principal hadn't "run interference" in this way, it is likely that inquiry would have fallen by the wayside. To argue that collaborative inquiry is nonlinear, thus, is *not* to say that it can withstand all of the obstacles that are set in its path. In fact, without a principal committed to inquiry as a primary form of professional development, collaborative inquiry stands little hope of surviving.

As teachers understand the potential powers of inquiry, they become savvier about what to put "on the table" and how to structure their meetings. In this case, the inquiry practice at Harbor evolves from a strict focus on student work in the first year and a half, to the inclusion of *teacher* work (in the form of curriculum plans, rubrics, assignment sheets, and so on) in the latter half of the project. As the teachers at Harbor became more experienced in inquiry, they made more strategic choices about the kinds of data sources that were likely to inform their investigations most powerfully. At first, the Evidence Project facilitator had led the way in suggesting what kinds of evidence to examine and what protocols to use to structure the conversations. It was an important turning point for the group when, in Phase 3, participating teachers took the initiative in determining which data to examine and in modifying the protocols used to examine them. The teachers had developed the capacity, in short, to identify their purposes for inquiry more precisely and to match their inquiry procedures to these purposes. Developing such capacity is an important milestone for any inquiry group.

The Melrose case, discussed in the following chapter, illustrates the work of a group of teachers that was quite practiced in taking this kind of initiative, and which used it, in this instance, to explore the benefits and pitfalls of a state-mandated reading curriculum.

Chapter 6

Engaging Equity and District Mandates: Inquiry at Melrose Elementary School

TOM MALARKEY

What does inquiry look like in a school where it has been practiced faculty-wide for a number of years? In this case study, we consider how Melrose Elementary School in Oakland, California, a school with an established culture of inquiry, is striving to deepen its inquiry work in order to affect more powerful changes in student learning, curriculum, and instruction. In this school, collaborative inquiry drives school-wide dialogue and decisions on critical issues and provides a powerful strategy for addressing equity issues facing the school.

This case focuses on one of the school's collaborative inquiry teams, the Sheltered English team, tracing its work over the course of 2 years. It highlights how, in its second year, the team critically engaged a district-mandated literacy curriculum through collaborative inquiry. The case describes how the school's approach to inquiry has evolved, enabling such work to occur, and considers how one team's inquiry can influence the school as a whole. It also illuminates the role an outside partner, the Bay Area Coalition for Equitable Schools (BayCES), has played in strengthening inquiry within the school. (For more information about BayCES and its Teacher Inquiry Project [TIP], see Chapter 3.)

THE SHELTERED ENGLISH TEAM'S FIRST YEAR OF INQUIRY

The Melrose Elementary School faculty, including counseling staff and instructional assistants, gathered in the cafeteria on an early release Wednesday in May. Once a month, the school's teachers had been meeting in their collaborative inquiry teams. However, this meeting was their annual culminating event of the year, at which the collaborative inquiry teams took turns presenting their questions and sharing with colleagues their "learnings" and some of the potential implications for other teachers and the whole school.

The sharing sessions functioned both as a celebration of work and as a forum for learning, as Melrose's principal, Moyra Contreras, put it in welcoming her faculty: "Every year we gather to hear what has been learned in these groups. It's very exciting. This is probably my favorite day in the whole year—besides Halloween!"

For the seven teachers on the Sheltered English inquiry team, planning for "going public" with their learnings in front of the school's faculty had helped to sharpen their thinking about the wider implications of their work. In a predominantly Latino school, the Sheltered English teachers faced a particular challenge. While the school had worked hard to create a Spanish bilingual program that addressed the specific needs of its majority Spanish–speaking population, it was less clear how the school was organizing itself to meet the specific needs of its African American and Southeast Asian students. To address this challenge, the team had focused its inquiry for the year on how to meet the English language development needs of all the cultural and linguistic groups in its classes. The term "Sheltered English" traditionally refers to an instructional approach for English-language learners that provides more support than "English immersion" typically does but is still in English. The Latino-majority schools in East Oakland often referred to their English-only nonbilingual classrooms as "Sheltered English," even when they included African American students, since there were few, if any, students for whom standard English was the home language.

At the presentation, the Sheltered English team members were excited to share what had been a powerful learning experience and, at the same time, nervous, since they would be raising some potentially controversial issues. They knew that for many of the teachers in the audience, the presentation would be the first unveiling of a detailed portrait of teaching and learning in the Sheltered English program.

Exploring English-Language Development and Parent Perceptions

Sue Jones, a White second-year teacher on the Sheltered team, began the presentation by sharing some of the team's initial questions, which had been captured on flipchart paper:

- Are African American and Southeast Asian students really struggling?
- How can I best support my African American and Southeast Asian students in their language needs?

- How do my students acquire language?
- How can I help them understand that their home language is good [i.e., culturally rich, to be valued]?
- What are the rates of turnover for the Sheltered students as compared with the Bilingual students?
- Why don't African American parents participate as other parents do?

Each member of the team then took a turn sharing a different aspect of the team's inquiry work from the year. In the course of their presentations, the teachers addressed both their initial questions and new ones raised in the course of the inquiry.

Teacher and team member Katie Thompson, a White fifth-year teacher, discussed how the team had looked at demographic and achievement data for their students, surfacing a gap between their students' reading scores on an authentic assessment and their significantly lower scores on the SAT9, the state's standardized assessment. Tarie Lewis, a White fifth-year teacher, reported on how she had piloted a new authentic assessment in her third-fourth-grade classroom that better approximated the kind of expository reading skills required on the SAT9. And Marla Kamiya, a Japanese American tenth-year kindergarten teacher, discussed inequities the team had observed that were specifically related to the African American and Southeast Asian families in the Sheltered program, including differing rates of parent participation in school events and the perception among some parents that the school was a "bilingual school" and not oriented toward their children—a perception that resulted in some parents' alienation from the school community.

Dorothy Cotton, a veteran African American teacher who had been at Melrose for 32 years, and Matt Behnke, a White third-year teacher, described the group's inquiry into how students' language and culture affected their learning. This led them to experiment with the Academic English Mastery Program (AEMP), a curriculum that focused on valuing students' home language, addressing particularly African American Language, while giving explicit instruction around "academic English," in order to build students' capacity to "code-switch" between these two languages and communicate successfully in both. Developed in Los Angeles by Noma Lemoine, AEMP's approach focused first on educating teachers about the linguistic structure of African American Language (AAL), the historical reasons for this structure, and the importance of seeing AAL as a "home language" for African American students. This philosophy was extended to other linguistic groups who were represented in Melrose's Sheltered English program—for example, Vietnamese, Mien, and Latino, groups that also used nonstandard forms of English.

Over the course of the year, the team had implemented key AEMP strategies in their classrooms, which they had individually selected. In her K–1 classroom, Terry Tasby, an African American second-year teacher, worked on creating ways for students to see their own cultures and languages represented in the curriculum (for example, African American and Latina astronauts), and in their classroom discourse: every day began with greetings from each of the seven languages spoken in the homes of children in the class. In their third- and fourth-grade classrooms, Tarie and Sue collaborated to create approaches to develop students' skills in contrastive analysis and link these code-switching literacy practices with social studies curricula about African American history and the historical development of African American language as shaped by slavery.

At the team's monthly inquiry group meetings, the teachers had shared their progress in these individual inquiries, sometimes presenting curriculum, other times sharing examples of student work. Since the individual inquiries were tied by common questions and concerns, the teachers' dialogue produced shared knowledge and strengthened their sense of professional community.

Impact of the Team's Inquiry on Their Teaching, Their Students, and Other Teachers

At the end of their year of inquiry, the teachers on the Sheltered English team were able to identify some significant outcomes for themselves and their students. For the teachers, the inquiry led to an appreciation of the importance of providing explicit instruction in English and provided them with a theory and shared vocabulary about language development to guide their instruction. It also led to changes in instruction and curriculum. For example, instead of "correcting" students when they used the "wrong" words or phrasing, the teachers focused on helping students to recognize the differences between academic English and their home languages, to translate between them, and to decide which language to use in which situations. Tarie reflected, "I'd struggled for years with a way to talk about standard English in a respectful way. If you're really going to talk about it, it's political. I didn't fully know how to do that—as a White teacher, as a newer teacher, and with third and fourth graders. Now I feel like my instruction is better because I have a way to talk about it, and they know what I'm talking about."

Most importantly, the teachers on the team began seeing different student results. Students were becoming more meta-cognitive in terms of their own language use, and showed improved scores on reading assessments. The team was especially gratified to see their students more freely sharing their own cultural backgrounds with one another, thus capitalizing on the diversity in the Sheltered classrooms.

Matt closed the team's end-of-year presentation that day in May by saying their work would continue. "This was actually a very hard presentation to organize—putting it all in order and telling the stories the right way. I guess we feel like we're halfway though something—well, we *know* we're halfway through something."

The presentation generated a great deal of discussion among the faculty about the strategies the Sheltered English team had begun to implement. Some of the bilingual teachers saw these strategies as potentially useful with their Spanish-speaking students. The presentation also spurred discussion of the equity issues facing non-Latino students and families in the school. As one bilingual teacher reflected later, "Hearing the Sheltered team raise issues of how Melrose students were not being well-served affected my inquiry the next year. It allowed me to explore and raise the issue of how our bilingual program was consistently not meeting the needs of certain students."

COLLABORATIVE INQUIRY AT MELROSE ELEMENTARY

How has Melrose's approach to inquiry enabled this kind of learning? Before picking up the story of the Sheltered English team's inquiry, it is important to present some background on inquiry at Melrose.

The school sits in a predominantly Latino and African American neighborhood in East Oakland. Its 500 students in grades K–5 reflect a shift in the community's demographics from predominantly African American to predominantly Latino: At the time of this writing, 80% are Latino, 15% African American, and 5% Southeast Asian and Pacific Islander. The school is one of the few in Oakland—and in the state—that still has a large bilingual Spanish-English education program. Roughly 75% of its students are enrolled in this program, while the remaining 25%—African American, Southeast Asian, and Latino—are enrolled in the Sheltered English program.

In a district where few schools have been able to mobilize coherent reform efforts from within, Melrose has sustained and deepened its reform work for almost a decade. Students in the school are generally grouped in multiage classrooms. The school has generally emphasized "progressive" pedagogy—for example, whole-language approaches to reading, process writing, and literature groups, though not all teachers fully endorse this philosophy. In recent years, the school has developed more targeted literacy strategies, such as Reciprocal Teaching and interventions such as Reading Recovery, and has piloted and adopted school-wide authentic reading assessments. While literacy levels at the school have been improving, many students still perform below grade level and fare poorly on statewide standardized tests.

A strong collaborative culture has developed at the school. Teachers meet regularly in grade-level teams, collaborative inquiry teams, and teacher-led governance committees, and the school is a district pilot for site-based management. Collaborative inquiry has become the backbone of professional development at the school. It has played a central role in introducing new curriculum and teaching strategies, building an assessment system, and raising larger issues of student learning and program articulation.

Melrose's principal of 8 years, Moyra Contreras, described the history of collaborative inquiry at the school this way:

> "Eight years ago we decided to construct our own professional development, instead of following the district's. It was important that teachers could have some choice in their professional learning. We tried several approaches, but teacher research groups wound up taking off. We decided to have everybody participate in those. We changed the name from 'research' to 'inquiry' and the [word] 'teacher' to 'collaborative' so that people other than teachers could participate."

Each year, all teachers at Melrose participate in collaborative inquiry. They are often joined by other certified staff. Collaborative inquiry topics shift year to year, allowing teachers to pursue collaborative learning about issues that are relevant at that time—both to themselves and to the school as a whole.

In September of each year, inquiry teams form around common areas of interest, and over the course of the year they meet monthly for 2 hours to learn together from individual and collective inquiry topics. At their first meeting, teachers share their interests and questions around the topic, and the team decides how it will use its time to support both individual and common work. In some cases, a team engages in jointly piloting a strategy or curriculum, such as reciprocal teaching, and learning how it plays out. In other cases, a team identifies a wider arena of interest, such as nonfiction writing, and the individual teachers pursue their own questions or approaches that are related to it, bringing their observations, data, and questions back to the team for discussion.

The cycle of inquiry typical of Melrose inquiry groups involves teachers taking conscious action in the classroom, collecting data on those actions, reflecting on the results, and making meaning through dialogue with colleagues—which, in turn, generates learning and new or refined action.

In some inquiry processes, teachers *begin* by gathering data around a question (for example, "Which students are not transitioning into English?"), then reflecting on that data and using it to drive subsequent action in their classrooms. Collaborative inquiry teams at Melrose did not generally employ formal structures such as protocols to discuss student or teacher work in their meetings, though some have begun to do this. Meetings typically shifted between teachers taking turns sharing their work and collective discussion of common issues. Most collaborative inquiry teams were also supported by the presence of an AmeriCorps member from Partners in School Innovation who helped with documentation and data organization.

The Sheltered English Team's Inquiry Process

Like other inquiry teams at Melrose, the Sheltered English team met once a month on early-release Wednesdays, when students are dismissed at 1:30 p.m. Fifteen minutes later, the teachers on the team would assemble, with somebody usually bringing snacks and drinks, in Tarie's third- and fourth-grade classroom. This was their preferred meeting place both because it was the most central location and because the chairs were higher than those in the K–2 classrooms!

Not only did the seven teachers span all the grade levels at Melrose, but they came from a variety of ethnic backgrounds and had a wide range of years teaching. This range of experience and perspectives was a critical resource for the group. As Tarie reflected, "I enjoy all the voices on our team, all the differing points of view. I like that it's a diverse group as far as age and backgrounds are concerned—bringing that together to focus on one particular goal, our children. I feel connected with them [the other teachers] in a very real way, and that had been missing for me."

Tom Malarkey, the school's coach from the Bay Area Coalition of Equitable Schools (BayCES), often joined the group. A White man in his second year working with the school, Tom provided general support, occasional facilitation, and various forms of documentation. Though the team had strong internal leadership, they welcomed an external presence, especially around challenging issues.

For the team, the meetings became a "space" that supported frank and difficult conversations about questions of equity surrounding the Sheltered English program and its place in the school. Examples of questions posed include, What kind of environment was Melrose for its non-Latino students and families, all of whom were in the Sheltered program? While the teachers came from different racial and economic backgrounds and had had different experiences at the school, they were all able to voice their feelings and concerns about these issues—issues that had polarized the staff in the past. As Dorothy, a veteran African American teacher, told the faculty during a presentation, "I've never really connected too well with collaborative inquiry before. But I love my group now. I feel I can talk about things that are real and that matter to me."

The structure of the Sheltered team's meetings differed from meeting to meeting. In part, this depended on the extent to which one or two teachers had taken the lead in organizing the meeting in advance. Sometimes they began with a clear agenda; other times the team negotiated their agenda at the beginning of the meeting. What was consistent about the team's meetings was that they covered a range of interconnected topics. The openness of the format allowed new issues connected to the day's topic to get taken up as they emerged.

In a typical meeting, the team's conversation would begin with individual teachers sharing examples of their practice that related to language development; for example, using "contrastive analysis" (from the Academic English Mastery Program curriculum), in which students "translate" between their home language and academic English. These discussions would be marked with questions from the other teachers about specific aspects of implementing the practice—"When," Why," and "How did you?" From there, the discussion would turn to one or more of the theoretical issues involved in language development—for example, the value of explicit instruction in a school with a history of whole-language instruction. Then the team would move to sharing and discussing results that teachers were seeing with their students—based on their own observations, student work samples, and scores from various assessments such as the Qualitative Reading Inventory (QRI). Positive results elicited comments such as "That's great!", "She has come so far this year!", and "I'd love to visit your class and see you do that." The teachers would then exchange ideas and develop strategies for what they wanted to try next.

At some point in the meeting, the conversation would shift from a focus on the teachers' own classroom practice within the Sheltered English program to a consideration of issues with wider implications for the school, such as what it means for African American and Southeast Asian students and families to be minorities within the school community. In these discussions, the teachers would share what they were learning from parents—both through informal conversations and more formal interviews. These conversations about school-wide concerns would often lead to talking about collective action—such as what issues they wanted to bring to the school's attention and how they might do this in one of the whole-faculty sharing sessions.

Leadership for the team's work tended to rotate among several teachers, who would do preplanning and organizing of materials and agenda for their meetings. This fluid model of leadership allowed energy to come from multiple sources. In a school engaged in complex reform work, which required significant teacher leadership, the myriad responsibilities could, at times, be exhausting for teachers. However, the importance of the Sheltered team's work and the strength of their relationships gave them added fuel. As Tarie reflected, "I feel like this group working together has been the most energy-producing of any group that I've worked with." When it was needed, the team asked for support in planning or facilitation from their BayCES coach.

ENGAGING WITH OPEN COURT:
THE SHELTERED ENGLISH TEAM'S SECOND YEAR OF INQUIRY

In the second year of their work together, the Sheltered team continued the various strands of their work, including implementation of strategies from AEMP described above, investigating parent connections, and further articulating a cross-grade continuum of Sheltered program instruction. In addition to this ongoing work, a new challenge had emerged for the school that affected the Sheltered teachers most immediately: How was the school going to respond to the district's new mandated literacy curriculum, Open Court? Published by SRA/McGraw-Hill, Open Court Reading is a literacy curriculum based on "systematic, explicit instruction of phonemic awareness, phonics and word knowledge, comprehension skills and strategies, inquiry skills and strategies, and writing and language arts skills and strategies." (Source: Homepage, SRA/McGraw-Hill website: *www.sra-4kids.com/product_info/ocr/*)

In the previous school year, the Oakland school district, along with others in the state, had mandated Open Court for all its elementary schools. Open Court is a highly scripted and sequenced curriculum that, if implemented fully, takes up significant portions of the instructional day. Its strong emphasis on phonics and decoding strategies runs counter to the whole-language, comprehension-oriented approaches valued by many Melrose teachers. Furthermore, the district required teachers' attendance at monthly Wednesday afternoon staff development meetings focused on implementing the new curriculum.

From the district's perspective, Open Court was a key equity strategy in a district where literacy levels were strikingly low, particularly for African American and Latino students, and few elementary schools had a coherent approach to literacy instruction. Even so, the Melrose faculty initially voiced serious concern. Would teachers be forced to scrap the literacy approaches they'd worked so hard to build? Would they lose control of their Wednesday afternoon professional development time due to the mandated Open Court training? As one Bilingual teacher put it, "We were panicked about it!"

Since a Spanish version of the curriculum was not yet ready, Melrose's Sheltered teachers were to be the first in the school to implement Open Court. The K–3 teachers had attended summer trainings and imagined they would be required to follow the lockstep implementation mandated by the district. However, Moyra Contreras, Melrose's principal, used the school's status as a site-based decision-making pilot in the district to take a different approach. She encouraged the Sheltered team to adopt an inquiry stance toward Open Court—that is, to study it, pilot the dimensions of the curriculum that seemed most important and that fit with their existing instructional approaches, and see what they could learn from it. As Katie reflected on Moyra's position, "She's been really open to it working. And she has told our team, 'You guys are professionals. You know what works and what doesn't work. But you need to be able to argue why.'"

That fall, the faculty as a whole decided that instead of attending the district's once-monthly staff development, they would use that time onsite for what they called "Literacy Articulation Wednesdays," or LAW. In October, they formed three LAW groups (K–2 Bilingual, 3–5 Bilingual, Sheltered English). In these groups, teachers shared literacy strategies, identified priorities, and worked toward a better articulation of the school's literacy program.

The Sheltered teachers used their LAW meetings, in essence, as additional collaborative inquiry time and focused their work on critically engaging Open Court to see where and how it might benefit their students and their literacy program. Their inquiry the year before, especially concerning the implementation of AEMP, had given them a rationale for why their students needed more explicit instruction in the rules of language ("academic English"), and they were more able to see the potential benefits of Open Court. In addition, they were clearer on the equity issues at stake: several in the group felt the school had historically overlooked the importance of decoding strategies and grammar instruction and how these specifically disadvantaged Melrose students, given that most were not getting strong exposure to literacy—and to academic English—at home.

The Team's Process for Inquiry into Open Court

To begin its inquiry, the team spent time understanding the theoretical and pedagogical underpinnings of Open Court. Katie and Tom planned the first LAW meeting in November. Katie had an idea that turned the usual approach to implementing curriculum upside down: rather than going through the scripted lessons, the team could organize their Open Court work around the appendix to the curriculum, which outlined the research behind Open Court and broke down the components of the literacy process.

The group decided that at each LAW meeting, they would address one realm of literacy instruction—writing, reading comprehension, phonics, classroom discussion, assessment. For each topic, the team members would discuss the practices they were already using, identify those they wanted to do more of, examine new practices from Open Court, and figure out how they would implement them. A key part of their plan was to use these discussions as a way to share what they had been doing at each grade level, identify gaps, and work to align their literacy curriculum across the grades. Planning and facilitation would rotate among the team members.

At the first meeting devoted to Open Court, the team dived into the phonics section. Each teacher wrote down on Post-its what he or she taught in phonics and how they taught it. These Post-its went up on a chart so the group could see the continuum across all six grades. Then Marla and Terry shared their kindergarten phonics instruction and the new practices they were using from Open Court. They reported that their students were already learning to read more quickly, and they were excited to see their kids' confidence growing as they mastered certain words and skills. Katie shared her work in "blending" (combining phonemic sounds to form a word) at the first-grade level, and Terry asked if she could visit her classroom to learn more about this. The group decided to identify for each grade level the skills to which students would be exposed and those they would be expected to master.

Results of the Inquiry

The inquiry into Open Court influenced students' and teachers' work in many ways. Some of the effects were immediate and tangible; other results emerged more slowly over time. An initial learning that surfaced in the inquiry meetings was that it was harder for the third- to fifth-grade teachers to keep on pace with the grade-level materials of Open Court since their students had not been exposed to that curriculum in the earlier grades. To address this, the teachers discussed what interventions might be needed to fill these gaps. The group also discovered that Open Court complemented many of the reading strategies they currently employed, such as Reciprocal Teaching. Teachers also realized that while their students' decoding strategies improved dramatically, students' comprehension strategies declined. As Katie reported to the faculty in their midyear inquiry sharing in March:

"What we have found out, for those of us doing Open Court, is that the phonics section in Open Court has been incredibly valuable—especially in the kindergarten, first grade, and some of second grade. That it's not only giving students a very systematic way of learning the sounds in English, but it's also giving them language to talk about English. With blending, I have noticed a significant increase in what my students can do in reading, having this phonics program. Unfortunately, the rest of the program, as we predicted, is not as strong. While my students can blend away, they really don't have a lot of fluency in their reading, and their comprehension has just tanked. And the literature is also a little too advanced—and often culturally inappropriate—for some of my students, and there isn't time built in for any kind of guided reading."

Seeing that a fuller implementation of Open Court tipped the balance too far away from comprehension, teachers like Katie could then adjust their practice and integrate literacy approaches like guided reading and Reciprocal Teaching, which had already been a successful part of their repertoires.

The inquiry into Open Court intentionally sought out ways to align and integrate different approaches, and so allowed teachers who came from different pedagogical (as well as cultural) backgrounds to engage these differences constructively. Each teacher's beliefs and practices changed in powerful—and very different—ways. Dorothy, the most veteran member of the team, had long believed in and practiced explicit phonics instruction, which put her in a minority among the school's faculty. Though she did not implement Open Court that year, discussing it with the others on her team gave her a way to share her practice, learn from what others were doing, and engage in deeper dialogue about instruction.

For the newer teachers, who came from the more progressive, constructivist teacher education programs at Mills College and the University of California at Berkeley, engaging Open Court sharpened their thinking about the role of explicit instruction and allowed them to experiment without feeling coerced. As Matt reflected during the planning for the team's presentation to the rest of the faculty, "I used to be such a whole language baby. Now, I'm all about pronouns! I'm loving grammar these days." It also gave all the Sheltered teachers a common instructional language, which, in turn, allowed them to share their classroom practices more freely over time.

The results for their students were evident as well. For example, Marla and Terry saw a significant increase in the number of kindergarteners who began reading that year, and Katie observed that her first and second graders had become much more confident in—and excited about—their reading. Furthermore, the Sheltered teachers saw gains on both standardized and authentic assessments. For example, Dorothy reported more fourth and fifth graders reading at grade level on the Qualitative Reading Inventory (QRI) used by the school. In general, across the grades, Melrose's African American students made the most improvements of any racial group on the SAT9 from the previous year.

Of course, one cannot attribute all these gains exclusively to the team's inquiry into Open Court. However, team members felt strongly that collectively developing more explicit approaches to literacy instruction and strategies that targeted the particular language needs of different groups of students influenced their students' learning. They looked forward hopefully to the future when, for instance, fourth graders would have had 3 consecutive years of consistent, rigorous literacy instruction—and wondered how much further students with this experience would travel by the end of their time in elementary school.

The Sheltered team's learning from inquiry—and their strengthened conviction about the importance of explicit instruction in language—spilled over to the rest of the faculty. The next section discusses how carefully considered changes in Melrose's collaborative inquiry structure enabled the team's learning to have an impact on the wider school.

FROM COLLABORATIVE INQUIRY TO ORGANIZATIONAL LEARNING

While collaborative inquiry is now a relatively stable and institutionalized structure at the school, the process is also constantly evolving, deepening, and becoming increasingly relevant. From being a "hit or miss" proposition for individual teachers several years ago, collaborative inquiry has become increasingly meaningful across the faculty, with more teachers deeply engaged in their own inquiry work and learning from the work of others.

Inquiry has come to be seen as an effective vehicle for wrestling publicly with difficult equity issues, such as understanding which groups of students the school has *not* served as effectively as others. Framing these challenges as questions, and grounding subsequent discussions in data, has allowed more constructive dialogue to occur on topics that have traditionally been difficult to discuss in other forums, such as faculty meetings.

Teachers' inquiry work has also become more formally linked to the school's decision-making processes—for example, using the knowledge created through inquiry to make informed decisions about curriculum development. In this regard, Melrose's inquiry process has also evolved in response to the district and state policy context, as the experience with Open Court demonstrates.

Several developments may account for this, including establishing a more centralized "planning and coordination" group; building the inquiry skills and leadership capacity of individual teachers (through involvement in outside networks); and using the resources provided by an outside partner. Tom, the school's BayCES coach, provided coaching for inquiry teams, helped create a more explicit structure for the school's process, and provided tools and information about how to approach inquiry.

One area upon which Tom had focused was how learning from one team could impact others in the school and influence the organizational learning of the school as a whole. In talking with teachers, reading their written reflections, and doing a set of interviews, he found that many teachers experienced a "disconnect" between their engaging, organic process and the required "products": the end-of-the-year presentations and required write-ups. Many felt the end-of-year presentations were more a performance than a real learning opportunity. Teachers also wanted to learn about each other's work before the end of the year when it was "done." Working with the school's Literacy Leadership Team and Management Team, which provided a loose oversight of the inquiry process, Tom helped the school develop two key changes in the process:

1. Collaborative inquiry sharing would also happen *during* the year, which allowed the school to act on issues that arose and enabled inquiry teams to receive feedback on their work in progress; and
2. The school would institute a process by which learnings and implications from collaborative inquiry could be more formally linked to key decision-making processes at the school—for example, planning of professional development, budgeting for the following year, strategic planning.

As a result of the first decision, the school added a collaborative inquiry sharing time in March. Teams were given the option to share in either March or May (or both). The March meeting was framed as sharing work in progress, not necessarily "findings." Tom encouraged teams to structure opportunities for discussion and small-group work as part of the presentations, and to present questions and challenges, not just learnings.

To implement the second decision, the faculty also decided that the Management Team would become the forum for discussing and acting upon the wider implications for the school that grew out of collaborative inquiry. The Budget Committee would also consider needs that emerged from collaborative inquiry in its decision making. Teachers felt that grounding such deliberations in learnings from their classrooms both honored their inquiry and was a sounder basis for decisions.

The School-Wide Effects of the Sheltered Team's Inquiry

The Sheltered team decided to use the newly instituted March inquiry presentations to share their second-year work-in-progress. They felt their learnings over several areas had implications for the school, and they wanted to put these on the table earlier in the year, so that the findings could inform dialogue and, possibly, promote action.

In their presentation, one of four at the meeting, the team shared learnings from their continuing implementation of AEMP strategies and modeled some of their teaching practices. They discussed efforts to engage Sheltered parents and to understand their perspectives through an initial set of interviews. They also highlighted the important role of instructional assistants and after-school staff in helping raise the profile of different student groups' cultures through events such as the Black History Month assembly. And, for the first time, they presented their early work piloting Open Court.

After giving a brief overview of the Open Court curriculum and the team's process, Katie modeled an interactive minilesson in blending for the rest of the teachers, asking them to call out the syllable sounds just as she would with her students. Her colleagues loved it. Katie went on to share the striking progress she saw her students make in their reading skills: first graders decoding text far more effectively—and enthusiastically—than she'd ever seen, choosing and reading higher-level texts, and demonstrating meta-cognition about their reading skills.

The Sheltered Team's presentation, especially the parts about their inquiry around AEMP and Open Court, contributed to shifting the dialogue at Melrose about the teaching of phonics and grammar. Influenced by the Sheltered teachers' enthusiasm and results, a number of the Bilingual teachers expressed interest in learning some of the key instructional strategies embedded in these curricula and investigated by the Sheltered team. Eventually, the school as a whole decided to adopt a focus on "Academic Language" for the following year, which included an increased emphasis on expository reading and writing skills and more explicit instruction in academic English, as modeled by the Sheltered team.

The Sheltered team's presentation on Open Court illuminates how, through the deliberate and thoughtful use of inquiry, what could have been an exercise in resistance and frustration became an opportunity to learn—

for the team and for the school. For the Sheltered team teachers, two outcomes from the school-wide sharing were particularly gratifying: The equity issues they discussed were now being taken up by other teachers in the school, and the needs of their students became a regular part of the discourse within the school.

While challenges remained, the school and the Sheltered English team had created a strong foundation from which to engage them seriously and openly. Learnings from other teams have also had real influence on the school. All realized now the impact that one group's work—within a school committed to deepening its approach to inquiry—could have. Reflecting on the Sheltered team, Marla said, "I think this group feels like there's a lot at stake. In our discussions and what we're doing, there are real consequences. I think that people feel like our work is important in the whole school—and that has changed everything."

COMMENTARY ON THE CASE

Inquiry helps teachers and administrators broach controversial topics. The Melrose case helps to illustrate what we believe is one of the greatest potential strengths of collaborative inquiry: It can provide a context for honest and productive discussions of controversial issues, issues that are often ignored or that might engender hostility and alienation among the faculty in schools that have not developed a culture of inquiry. It is never easy to talk about equity issues, nor to explore ideologically opposed approaches to pedagogy. But the teachers at Melrose knew that their "inquiry stance" would help them get beyond silence or potential shouting matches: asking clear, specific questions and collecting tangible data would provide a framework for discussion that would make it possible to broach tough issues and to gain new insights into them.

Inquiry into a mandated curriculum provides a striking opportunity for and expression of professionalism. We noted previously that, in addition to exploring controversial issues, inquiry groups often use their research efforts as an opportunity to reflect on other teaching initiatives. This is borne out here, as the Melrose teachers explored the Open Court curriculum. It is worth highlighting that the use of Open Court was mandated from above, by the state—and that Open Court itself requires highly structured, explicit instruction, rather than a more progressive or constructivist pedagogy. Exposing Open Court to inquiry, thus, the teachers powerfully assert their professional judgment and decision-making capacity. In a situation in which they might have simply done as they were told, the teachers at Melrose held onto the conviction that they, the people closest to their students, were in the best position to see what works for them. They would certainly take what the externally developed curriculum had to offer—but they would not defer their professional expertise to others.

An outside support provider plays a role, even at a site with long experience in inquiry. Funders and others who are concerned about the sustainability of a collaborative inquiry endeavor are often tempted to think that ultimately, all guidance and support for the inquiry process might come from within a school. This book is written by outside support providers, so this is not a point about which we can claim disinterest. And yet it is worth noting that even at Melrose, where inquiry had been an integral part of school practice for 8 years, the outside coach played an important role in helping teachers develop new processes for sharing their learning across the school and in linking findings from collaborative inquiry to the school's decision-making processes. In this case and the others, the outside coach also offered facilitation support and crucial networking opportunities with other schools engaged in similar work. For schools embarking upon or deepening their practice of collaborative inquiry, it is worth considering the role an outside support provider might play.

Part III

Toward a Culture
of Inquiry

The two chapters in this section generalize from the cases presented in the previous part to provide insight into the critical milestones in establishing and deepening inquiry and to outline policy issues and directions for future research. Chapter 7 outlines significant milestones, or key moments, gleaned from the four cases presented, and consistent with other documented cases of inquiry, which signal a movement or shift in the inquiry toward its specific purposes and the goal of supporting improved student learning and understanding. Sometimes participants in inquiry will recognize a significant milestone as it is achieved; others will become apparent only in retrospect, through reflection and documentation of the group's work.

No one milestone, in and of itself, equals effective collaborative inquiry; but together the milestones provide a framework for thinking about what matters most in developing effective collaborative inquiry groups. This chapter also summarizes the transformations that occurred for individual teachers and groups of teachers as they moved from the initial and tentative attempts to define their questions to realizing that the "loop" had been closed between their inquiry group and the classroom—a moment when they could see student successes that were a direct result of the inquiry process.

The final chapter returns to the theme of Chapter 1, namely, the inextricable link between teacher and student learning; it contends that, without the former, the latter cannot occur, and that collaborative inquiry groups play a potentially powerful role in developing and sustaining a culture of learning among teachers in schools. The chapter explores the policy and research questions that must be addressed if education systems take seriously the proposition that teachers are valued professionals with the capacity to develop and research the knowledge needed to foster their own learning and that of their students. Currently the practice of collaborative inquiry is ad hoc and dependent on the foresight, initiative, and knowledge of individual teachers, principals, and district staff. The chapter suggests that in order for the promise of inquiry to expand and reach more schools and students, significant questions for researchers remain, including the link between teacher and student learning, the potential for inquiry to support greater equity in students' opportunity to learn, and the ways in which designs for inquiry can help groups achieve the milestones that signal its effectiveness. Deeper understanding of these and other questions will be enhanced as the practice of inquiry becomes more prevalent and there is a sufficient depth and breadth of experience with inquiry to conduct rigorous and ongoing research.

Chapter 7

Milestones and Discoveries: A Cross-Case Commentary

The metaphor of the inquiry table, introduced in Chapter 2, helps us discuss crucial aspects of the collaborative inquiry process—and only partly because the work usually happens around a table! As we have seen in the cases presented in Chapters 3 through 6, who is at the table, what is on the table, what is done at the table, and how the table is supported are all important questions for consideration in planning this work. At this point, however, it will be useful to suggest a different metaphor, for, in many ways, as the cases illustrate, collaborative inquiry begs to be discussed as a journey—or, perhaps, borrowing from the practice of The Harbor School, as a learning expedition. This metaphor allows us to appreciate and discuss the senses of movement and exploration that are so central to this work. In particular, as we take a brief look back across all of the cases, we highlight potential milestones and discoveries that mark the path of collaborative inquiry.

DEVELOPMENTAL MILESTONES

Our research is too preliminary to present a "map of milestones"—and, in any case, it is likely that milestones vary somewhat from group to group. Our collective experience, however, suggests that at least some milestones are predictable, necessary points on the road to increased effectiveness in collaborative inquiry. We present them for the guidance they might offer to others exploring this terrain.

Finding the "right" questions. Elena's question—"How do I help my students to become young people who enjoy reading enough to choose it for recreation or a pleasurable way to spend time?"—is so directly connected to her own passion for reading that the question might appear to have written itself (see Chapter 3). However, for most groups of teachers, finding a generative question or set of questions requires the rare commodities of time and support. The questions tend to start out too general or too narrow—or maybe are not formulated in a way that could be addressed by empirical data (see Chapter 5). When a group reaches the point that it feels it has found the right question—at least for the time being—it has achieved an important milestone. Having formulated a powerful question not only allows a group to proceed in its cycle of inquiry, through data collection and the rest; it also positions teachers in an "inquiry stance," discussed in the commentary on Chapter 3, in which the heart and mind are more open to possibilities and discovery.

   "Going public" with classroom artifacts. Recognizing the challenge of sharing student work from one's own classroom, the Academy for Educational Development introduced the Reviewing Student Work project by having teachers examine student work from an outside source (Chapter 4). Maxson Middle School teachers later made the leap, with some trepidation, to sharing their own and their students' work both with colleagues and with other educators, at cross-school reviews. Teachers have long swapped worksheets and assignments to help one another plan lessons. But one cannot overstate the extent to which sharing one's own work and one's students' work, for the purpose of collaborative critical reflection and dialogue, breaks the norms of current school practice (Little, Gearhart, Curry, & Kafka, forthcoming). As we argued in Chapter 1, such a substantive change in norms requires conscious attention to trust-building, and the process takes time. One can see such trust developing, though, as teachers take a deep breath, open their manila folders, and share their work.

   The willingness to share one's work with colleagues can have, as we have seen, powerful analogies in the classroom—for trust is also a crucial ingredient in thriving classrooms. Experiencing the power of collaborative learning themselves, teachers draw tools from the inquiry work to support students in sharing their work, revealing their uncertainties, and offering honest feedback to each other. Because such sharing contributes so powerfully to learning, each step in building trust—both among teachers and students—is an appreciable milestone.

   "Taking ownership" to shape and monitor the inquiry process. In all of our cases, with the exception of Melrose Elementary (Chapter 6), inquiry was introduced by an outside organization with expertise in this area. It is natural, under such circumstances, that teachers new to collaborative inquiry would defer to the expertise of the outsiders, relying on their facilitation and their choices of protocols and data sources, taking cues from them about how to formulate questions, use protocols and other tools, and the like. As the groups develop, however, they take over more of these roles,

as we saw, for example, at The Harbor School (Chapter 5), where teachers began to take on facilitation of the group and to modify the structure of the meetings.

There is a kind of leap of imagination that occurs here, when teacher inquirers see how to take the tools of inquiry and apply them to their unique questions and sets of circumstances. It's probably not unlike a novice cook who, having followed many recipes, one day closes the cookbook and invents a new dish. This kind of milestone manifests itself in many ways—from bringing an important piece of research to the group that is relevant to their students to the reconfiguration of an inquiry group; from a decision about how to present findings to an insight about the implications of the inquiry for practice. When a group feels sufficient confidence to chart its course more consciously and independently, it's a milestone worth celebrating.

Addressing issues of equity through inquiry. At The Harbor School, teachers began by bringing the most impressive samples of student work to the table and slowly transitioned to bringing less successful pieces (Chapter 5). The willingness to bring less successful work signals that a group has developed a greater sense of trust, of course. But it also signals that the group is ready to take on issues that are particularly difficult to discuss. Naturally, bringing "lower-end" work raises questions about the expectations teachers have for the students who have produced this work and about the opportunities they are given in the classroom and by the school. In a word, "lower-end" work raises questions about equity and the distribution of resources—vexing, heated issues in any context. Raising these questions can be even more heated and complex when, as at Melrose, teachers and their students represent a diversity of races and ethnicities and have divergent perspectives on questions of institutionalized racism, gender bias, and the like.

If broaching these issues is challenging, it also has the potential for tremendous benefits. We can see that the readiness to look at all students' work—not just the stellar examples—allows teachers to ask, as those at Melrose did (Chapter 6), how to meet the needs of students who are particularly struggling. This question can lead to growing awareness on the part of teachers that to meet the needs of struggling students, some significant changes in school design or instruction might be called for. A willingness to look at work from struggling students and to engage in the questions of equity raised by that work, then, seems to us a crucial landmark on the way to our final milestone—"closing the loop."

"Closing the loop" for classroom and school-wide practice. As we have argued throughout this book, we believe that the ultimate aim of

collaborative inquiry is to help teachers become more skillful at their craft. We have pointed out several instances where the fact of engaging inquiry itself has seemed to improve teaching—at Maxson (Chapter 4), where teachers wove reflection on learning more consciously and directly into assignments; and at Melrose (Chapter 6), where teachers' inquiry into the Academic English Mastery Program helped them to help their students become more aware of "code-switching." For inquiry to be effective, it is essential to close the loop between what is learned around the table and what happens in the classroom. The moment when teachers see the impact of their inquiry on their practice (or on the practice of the whole school) is a major milestone, indeed.

Discoveries and Transformations on the Way

The appeal of a learning expedition is not only milestones or markers of progress, but also the discoveries and even personal transformations that occur on the journey. Collaborative inquiry offers the possibility for some of these, as well. Here are some discoveries and transformations that our cases illustrate:

A greater sense of efficacy for teachers coupled with improved outcomes for students. After the ASCEND case (Chapter 3), we commented on the impact of inquiry on Elena's sense of efficacy—based on her observations of students' growth in their enthusiasm about reading. This theme carries through all of the cases: in the Maxson case (Chapter 4), Miriam felt that she had become much more adept, through her inquiry, at helping her students understand their own learning processes more deeply. At Harbor (Chapter 5), new teachers "found out what they needed to be doing" in the principal's phrase—and experienced teachers saw their students "take charge of their own learning" in new ways. At Melrose (Chapter 6), teachers bridged the often unbridgeable gap among schools of thought on teaching reading, and found ways to combine phonics and whole-language approaches that proved highly effective for their students. As student skills improved, so did the teachers' sense of their own ability to contribute to their students' growth.

A lens for examining and adopting the best of reform and curricular initiatives. We have noted that collaborative inquiry provided teachers in these cases with a venue and a method for reflecting on curricular or reform initiatives (either mandated or voluntary)—the state reading standards at ASCEND, America's Choice at Maxson, Expeditionary Learning at Harbor, and Open Court at Melrose. As long as schools abound with new curricula and new approaches to pedagogy—a trend that shows no signs of waning—teachers benefit immediately from having a forum and a set of procedures that help them think critically about these new initiatives.

Engaging in inquiry makes room for teachers to approach their work with an open mind and to change their opinions and approaches, when necessary. Recall Matt from Melrose (Chapter 6): "I used to be such a whole-language baby. Now, I'm all about pronouns! I'm loving grammar these days!" Inquiry helps teachers to find ways of integrating important elements of new initiatives—rather than to "wait it out," as is so tempting when one gets hit by wave after wave of reform.

A method for addressing both personal teaching challenges and school-wide practices and decision-making. Elena's story (Chapter 3) illustrates why a teacher might engage in inquiry more or less on her own. Just focusing on a question that mattered to her provided her with insights into her students and her teaching and helped her avoid discouragement and despair. Certainly, an individual teacher (in this case, with a thoughtful and experienced e-mail buddy) might address individual teaching challenges through inquiry. But as the evolution of Elena's story and the launching of inquiry at ASCEND bear out, collaborative inquiry holds the potential of contributing more than the sum of the parts.

Collaborative inquiry does not simply bring together a number of individuals to talk about their individual inquiries. Collaborative inquiry also allows school faculties to uncover and address their collective challenges and to affect school policy. We see this collective impact in the other cases—at Harbor (Chapter 5), for example, with the growing shared understanding of what constitutes a high-quality learning expedition, and at Melrose (Chapter 6), with deepened understanding of the language needs of African American and Asian students.

In introducing the cases of inquiry presented here, we noted that we hoped to convey the look and feel of what it is like to be engaged in collaborative inquiry. Beyond this visceral sense, these cases have illustrated some of the notable milestones and discoveries that reward participants in collaborative inquiry and their students. Schools like ASCEND, Maxson, Harbor, and Melrose, are charting a new course. We hope that their stories will help other schools reach their own milestones and make their own discoveries through collaborative inquiry.

Chapter 8

Toward a Culture of Inquiry: Reflections and Policy Implications

In *The Predictable Failure of Educational Reform* (1993), Seymour Sarason wrote, "it is virtually impossible to create and sustain over time conditions for productive learning for students when they do not exist for teachers" (p. 145). While this is not the only reason Sarason cites for the "predictable failure" of efforts to substantially improve our nation's schools, he is pointing to perhaps the sine qua non of school improvement—that schools must become genuine environments for learning. But Sarason goes further than many who make this obvious statement and draws a conditional connection between teacher learning and student learning.

In the absence of a school culture in which there is an expectation that all teachers will remain learners—about their subject matter, about their students as human beings, about the delicate craft of teaching and the human phenomenon of learning—there is little chance that all students will become learners of the things we believe they need to know or even the things they themselves want to learn. And, overwhelmingly, our public schools fail to nurture that culture of professional learning. Indeed, spending a day, or even an hour, in many schools raises the question of whether we have created cultures of learning—let alone of deep, thoughtful and thought-provoking study—for anyone, adults or children.

The case studies and analysis in this book underscore Sarason's belief that opportunities for teacher learning are inextricably linked to the potential for student learning. This is the ultimate source of the argument for creating a culture of inquiry for teachers—that it is the foundation of a similar culture for students. The movement, fledgling as it most often seems, to create situations for genuine and rigorous learning through inquiry (and not a few hours of lecture during an in-service day or "training" in a new teaching technique) draws its urgency from the same source as most other efforts at school improvement—the desire to improve the learning experiences and outcomes for students.

AN INVITATION TO JOIN IN INQUIRY

Noted Canadian authority on children's literacy Frank Smith has argued that children learn to read and write from adults who seem to value and enjoy the acts of reading and writing. These adults, sometimes formal and sometimes informal teachers, "invite" these young people into the "literacy club," a club they have chosen to join, in turn serving as mentors, coaches, collaborators, and inspirations to new members:

> Good teachers . . . manifest attitudes and behaviors that learners become interested in manifesting themselves, and then these teachers help learners to manifest such attitudes and behaviors for themselves. . . . The two essential characteristics of all the good teachers I have met is that they are interested in what they teach and they enjoy working with learners. Indeed, they are learners themselves. (p. 171)

Throughout this book we have spoken of inquiry groups, but we might expand our image of these groups and borrow Smith's point about clubs. The work of inquiry, for children or adults, becomes especially attractive when we see others whom we respect engaged in it. While in some schools inquiry groups are mandatory and in others they are voluntary, genuine engagement in the work comes when members truly "join in" the spirit of the work. At that point, inquiry becomes infectious and a part of the definition of who we are as teachers and learners.

In this regard, the story of Elena Aguilar's inquiry in the ASCEND case study (Chapter 3) highlights the possibilities inherent in engaging students directly in the active research of her inquiry. Elena went straight to her students for insight and information, drawing them in to understand their relationship to reading. Elena invited her students to join with her in this inquiry. She understood and communicated to her students that she needed and wanted their collaboration. And as they provided clues to the puzzle, they became her colleagues, transforming the traditional "battle lines" so often drawn between students and teachers. They became partners in the quest to develop understanding through inquiry.

In this way, too, Elena has made explicit a kind of meta-curriculum. She has drawn her students into a reflective analysis of themselves as readers and learners. Many in the field of education recognize the critical importance of engaging students in "learning how to learn." The trajectories of the formal, subject matter curriculum and the meta-curriculum are intricately intertwined. As teachers, we must teach content, but we must also teach ways of getting inside the content, exploring it, making sense of it, and working with it. Elena found, quite easily and instinctively, a way to invite her students to take an "inquiry stance" toward their own learning and, in so doing, both she and her students were immediate beneficiaries.

In schools, those who take an inquiry stance are always working on developing deeper understanding of their subject matter, but they are also struggling to understand the mysteries and complexities of learning and teaching. They'll stay late after school or gather on the weekend. They read articles and books and engage others in their explorations, seeking any clues to their puzzle. They welcome insight from any source and do not hesitate to reveal their confusions. They are addicted to what the late Nobel physicist Richard Feynmann called "the pleasure of finding things out."

Professionalism and an Inquiry Stance

All professionals are expected to account for their performance. In fact, one of the hallmarks of a profession is a forum established for the critical appraisal of and explication of one's actions. The professional teacher in public schools has precious few settings for providing this kind of account. Indeed, many teachers have so little practice in explaining their choices, actions, and assessments that they are often uncomfortable when called upon to do so.

Though the case studies in this book describe diverse approaches to collaborative inquiry in schools, the common themes running through all of them might be expressed in three basic questions:

- Why do we do what we do?
- Why do we do it in the way we do it?
- How might we do it better?

These questions are asked and explored in a variety of ways by these different groups, but they represent, for all of them, both a focus for the groups' work and a step toward reclaiming a degree of professionalism and responsibility that is lacking in far too many schools. In schools that take this step (and in all of the schools discussed in this book), "teacher accountability" is coming to be understood as the responsibility to understand how and why deep learning is (or isn't) taking place in one's classroom and how to make it happen more often and more deeply. It is this introspective, probing creation of a professional knowledge base that, more than external mandates, will obligate educators to respond to students' learning needs with rigor and compassion.

The Path from Insight to Action

A reasonable concern—and a common criticism—of inquiry groups in schools is that they are simply settings in which questions are raised, but never answered, and that they lead to little substantive change or improvement. Critics would argue that this inquiry stuff is just so much "navel gazing."

Indeed, it is quite possible that reflection and inquiry into such difficult work as teaching, the complexities of schooling, and the challenges of learning will not cut through the confusions, assumptions, and beliefs that prevent the breakthroughs that lead to new possibilities. And even though serious conversation in an after-school meeting may lead to a new insight, it may not suggest the actions that will make a difference in student learning. The path from insight to action is itself fraught with obstacles. So what is the source of our confidence that these inquiry groups will lead to improved teaching and learning?

First, as the cases in this book bear out, we have heard from educators and seen in their work the ways in which understandings generated through inquiry lead to improvements in how teachers engage students in learning on a day-to-day basis in the classroom. Teachers, through inquiry, do move toward the strategies and stances that we know, through decades of research carried out by our organizations and others, lead to better student learning. These changes don't come easily—a fact also borne out by the cases in this book. Confusions, struggles, and barriers abound. Yet some schools have managed to negotiate those obstacles, supporting inquiry as it needs to be supported in order for it to lead to improvements for teachers and students.

There is another reason for our confidence and our commitment. We are convinced that institutionalized and well-supported opportunities for reflection and inquiry offer schools the best opportunity—perhaps the only real opportunity—to break the pattern of lurching from one ineffective "quick fix" to another, a pattern to which so many schools fall prey.

John Dewey, in his essay "Why Reflective Thinking Must Be an Educational Aim," wrote in 1933 on the relation of reflection to action. His comments remind us that though thoughtful action is not assured with reflective thinking, it can hardly be expected in its absence:

We all acknowledge, in words at least, that ability to think is highly important; it is regarded as the distinguishing power that marks man off from the lower animals. But since our ordinary notions of how and why thinking is important are vague, it is worthwhile to state explicitly the values possessed by reflective thought. In the first place, it emancipates us from merely impulsive and merely routine activity. Put in positive terms, thinking enables us to direct our activities with foresight and to plan according to ends-in-view, or purposes of which we are aware. It enables us to act in deliberate and intentional fashion to attain future objects or to come into command of what is now distant and lacking. By putting the consequences of different ways and lines of action before the mind, it enables us to *know what we are about when we act. It converts action that is merely appetitive, blind, and impulsive into intelligent action.* (1974, p. 212, italics in original)

"To know what we are about when we act" could be the inscription written above the doorway of every inquiry group in every school.

AGAINST ALL ODDS: TOWARD A CULTURE OF INQUIRY

Throughout this book, the authors have identified challenges to establishing and sustaining inquiry groups in our public schools. These have included, among others, extremely limited time and resources for collegial and collaborative work, the pressures of a mandated curriculum, the imposition of high-stakes standardized testing, the tradition of individualism among teachers, and the accelerating and often baffling pace of change in our world. As this book goes to press, states and school districts across the United States are grappling with unprecedented budget cuts. In short, expectations for the performance of students and teachers are rising while resources are vanishing. In this context, simply keeping school doors open becomes a challenge, let alone building rich, powerful learning environments for children and adults.

The work described in this book does not address all of the policy issues involved in the large social project to make our schools adequate to the task assigned to them—the education to high levels of each child, across all lines of race, gender, language, and class. It does, however, take on the deep and persistent problem that very little policy debate ever directly addresses—how to nurture and support the professional and intellectual lives of teachers. If the learning of students is inextricably linked to the learning of their teachers, what would policies that take this connection seriously look like? What might it take to support collaborative inquiry on a wide scale in our schools?

Most of the cases reported in this book represent inquiry in its early stages of development. And while we maintain a critical skepticism about the work, our commitment to its importance has only deepened through our engagement with educators and schools like those portrayed in this book. That commitment—tempered by cautious optimism in an uncertain policy context—leads us to outline some of the key questions that need to be explored and central issues that policy must address if serious work in the field of collaborative inquiry is to be nurtured in schools.

THE PRACTICE OF INQUIRY: THE CHALLENGES OF GOING DEEPER AND BROADER

Two fundamental challenges face the kind of inquiry work described in this book. The first is to go broader, pushing in the realms of policy and organization (of schools and districts) to make collaborative inquiry a supported and protected part of professional life in all schools. This means doing things such as allocating money from school budgets to support teachers' time as well as the coaches, facilitators, and outside partners who must join teachers in this work. The current reshaping of public schools, especially the move to create more small and personalized learning communities, provides an important opportunity to reconsider the professional and intellectual lives of teachers. The success of these new structures depends upon rethinking how teachers communicate and collaborate with each other and with others invested in students' academic achievement.

The second challenge is to probe more deeply into the possibilities and problems inherent in the work of inquiry under what are currently the best possible conditions—reasonably adequate time and resources, administrative support, a willing group of teachers, and so on. For example, the problem of moving from insight to action is critical in the long work of making collaborative inquiry efforts fulfill their potential to serve as a primary means of improving the quality of learning and teaching. Studying inquiry carried out under the best conditions is essential to learning how to do this work at the highest levels. The results of those investigations will provide all those interested in the potential of inquiry with images of what the work can look like, what it can make possible, and a clearer sense of what it takes to fulfill that potential.

The authors of this book look forward to the time when we will be able to look back on the questions and issues raised here as those of novices just starting on the path toward a far more sophisticated understanding of the elements of successful inquiry work in schools. At this point, though, we are clear about some of the areas in which immediate attention can strengthen and deepen this kind of work in schools. We name five of these areas below.

What Is the Link Between Teacher Inquiry and Student Inquiry?

As noted earlier in this chapter, creating more explicit links between teacher inquiry and student inquiry is one way to ensure that there is a connection between what teachers do in these groups and how students benefit from that work. Again, Elena Aguilar's work from the ASCEND case study (Chapter 3) is a strong example of this connection. Another appears in the work of The Harbor School (Chapter 5), where Joe Zaremba used the approaches of his inquiry group in his classroom, enabling his students to identify their own questions about their work, gather feedback from their peers and, ultimately, become the arbiters of the quality of their own efforts. Miriam Malabanan's work with her students to reflect more deeply on their learning at the same time that she and the members of the MIT sixth-grade team asked themselves how they could reflect more deeply on their students' work (Chapter 4) represents another example.

What Is the Link Between Inquiry and Equity?

Central to the work of any inquiry group has to be the educational welfare of all children in the school community. While there are many potential starting points for the work of an inquiry group, perhaps the most compelling is to ask which students—as groups and as individuals—are not having the best possible educational experiences in the school. This may well be in terms of academic achievement. At the same time, it could also be in relation to other factors, such as full integration into the social life of the school, access to college counseling and other forms of planning for the future, or opportunities for self-expression and participation in the cultural life of the school community. The enhancement of self-knowledge, such as the process of inquiry affords, often helps educators look differently and perhaps more accurately upon the needs of their students.

Who Will Be the Champions of Inquiry?

Starting and sustaining inquiry groups in schools requires a set of skills and experiences possessed by few people currently working in schools. While the cases in this book describe inquiry groups in which partners from outside the school played a substantive role, the long-term and widespread creation of inquiry groups in schools across the country will require a new cadre of internal and external facilitators, as well as teacher leaders and administrators to nurture the work. Identifying the necessary skills and understandings and figuring out where, when, how, and who to help develop them is a critical next step in advancing this work.

What Are the Best Designs for Inquiry?

One of the many questions raised in this book concerns the diversity of approaches to inquiry taken by our three organizations. To what degree do the differences in these approaches make a significant difference in the outcomes of the work? In short, which differences make the most difference? This remains, for us, another area needing further investigation. We do know that any attempt to create an inquiry group is, in effect, a design process. As in any subtle design process, the particularities of each setting must be carefully weighed, considered, and taken into account. In this way, considerable "custom work" will be called for, while there may also be considerable borrowing of elements used successfully in other settings.

Identifying and becoming sensitive to indicators that a design is working or not is another area of need. The "champions" of this work must be able to sense and assess when a group is engaged in a process that is leading to understanding, growth, and positive actions and changes in the classroom.

What Are the Milestones of Inquiry?

The pace of inquiry, while sometimes leading quite quickly to new ideas, insights, and actions, can also be slow. A group of teachers can work on a single question for months before feeling that they are making progress. Is this an impossibly slow pace or simply what is required to do serious work on difficult problems? Most research done in universities takes, by school standards, far too long to yield findings or results. Should we expect that a group of teachers, often meeting just about an hour once or twice a month, will untie the knots of teaching and learning in only a few meetings?

Learning the milestones of inquiry is, then, another challenge that is crucial to assessing the design of the process. The cases in this book suggest some possible milestones, described more fully in the previous chapter; for example, teachers' developing the norm of bringing to the table the less-than-stellar work from their students and themselves (as in the Maxson case study in Chapter 4), or an increase in teachers' ability to monitor and shape their own inquiry (as in The Harbor School in Chapter 5). In any long and complex journey, knowing some predictable milestones can help us determine when we are truly lost or when we are simply going through unfamiliar territory. As we struggle to develop sophistication in this work and with these processes, we must not only develop a strong sense for where we are at any point, but also be able to describe to others the significance of the milestones we approach and pass.

Further, the pace of building a culture of inquiry in a school can be painfully slow, and those who would guide and protect that process must have both great confidence and a broad perspective to be able to see progress, regress, or stasis. Again, most of the "champions" of this work have many decisions to make and, at this point, not all that much experience or information upon which to base those decisions. Also, celebrating milestones in inquiry work can provide the impetus to go further. Therefore, continuing to research and catalog the milestones, as we have begun to do here, should contribute to building our collective ability to track the progress of inquiry work.

How Can We Go Broader and Deeper at the Same Time?

In short, in order to go broader in meaningful and robust ways, we must continue to build on all we have learned about what makes these practices powerful. Similarly, without policies that support these practices, the kind of inquiry groups we have described will remain hothouse flowers, needing special conditions to survive. Fortunately, several recent developments contribute to our confidence that we are at a propitious moment for "growing" inquiry in schools.

As noted previously, the movement toward the creation of small schools and other alternative structures within existing schools provides a moment for those designing these schools and for district officials to fully consider what inquiry work requires. Time, of course, is key, but as the school schedule is being reconsidered, it is possible to draw on the solutions that some schools have invented for creating the time and space for teachers to meet and ask themselves tough questions (see Chapter 2). Human resources are needed, too, notably people with expertise in facilitating inquiry. Again, as roles and responsibilities, even basic practices, such as supervision and evaluation, are being reconceptualized in the design of new or restructured schools, this is a moment to create new positions, new budget lines, and new expectations for what it means to be a teacher.

The emergence of a new generation of teachers also provides a critical opportunity to redefine our image of a teacher. In this regard, schools of education also have a crucial role to play in inviting their students to engage in wondering, questioning, studying student work, observing students at work, and analyzing what makes learning happen. Indeed, an inquiry stance stands to enrich the quality of thought and practice of preservice and in-service teachers and administrators in every aspect of their education and development.

THE VALUES OF INQUIRY AND ITS VALUE

An intellectual life is built on interest and engagement in matters of complexity and significance. Human learning is such a matter, and those who love learning, find it fascinating, and seek both to understand it and nurture it in others are teachers. In the field of education, we believe we can, in time and with effort, better understand the interaction among people that is learning and teaching. Furthermore, we believe that we can turn that understanding into the creation of more effective environments and situations for learners of all ages.

A central premise of this book and of the inclination to establish collaborative inquiry among teachers in schools is that teachers are fully capable and, in many ways, uniquely situated to achieve these new understandings and invent more effective teaching practices. They need all the help they can get, of course. But they don't need someone else to do all of that work for them. In the end, no one can do the work of understanding and invention for anyone else, though we all benefit from the insights of others and can, through collaboration, often solve problems and design new practices that we could barely approach on our own.

Absent a deep respect for both students and teachers, for the subject matter, and for the processes of learning and teaching, there is little reason to expect significant progress in the improvement of schools. It is precisely these forms of respect we have seen developing in the schools in which we have been exploring the possibilities and puzzles of inquiry work. We have seen it in the deepening and strengthening of teachers' understandings of their work and their students' learning, and in a sense of professional renewal and respect that are both the foundation of any educational process and among the central goals of those processes as well. We hope this book makes visible what we have witnessed in the past few years—the potential and the beauty of collaborative inquiry in schools.

References

Academy for Educational Development. (2002a). *National Writing Project: Year two evaluation report*. New York: Author.

Academy for Educational Development (2002b). *School self-assessment: An inquiry-based approach to school improvement*. New York: Author.

Allen, D. (Ed.). (1998). *Assessing student learning: From grading to understanding*. New York: Teachers College Press.

Allen, L. A., & Calhoun, E. F. (1998). Schoolwide action research: Findings from six years of study. *Phi Delta Kappan, 78*(9), 706–710.

Ancess, J. (1996). *Outside/inside, inside/outside*. New York: National Center for Restructuring Education, Schools and Teaching, Teachers College.

Argyris, C., & Schön, D. A. (1978). *Organizational learning: A theory of action perspective*. New York: McGraw Hill

Ball, D. L., & Cohen, D. K. (1999). Developing practice, developing practitioners: Toward a practice-based theory of professional education. In L. Darling-Hammond & G. Sykes (Eds.), *Teaching as the learning profession: Handbook of policy and practice* (pp. 3–32). San Francisco: Jossey-Bass.

Bray, J. N., Lee, J., Smith, L. L., & Yorks, L. (2000). *Collaborative inquiry in practice: Action, reflection, and meaning making*. Thousand Oaks, CA: Sage Publications.

Brown, A. L., & Campione, J. C. (1994). Guided discovery in a community of learners. In K. McGilly (Ed.), *Classroom lessons: Integrating cognitive theory and classroom practices* (pp. 229–270). Cambridge, MA: MIT Press.

Bryk, A. S., & Schneider, B. (2002). *Trust in schools: A core resource for improvement*. New York: Russell Sage Foundation.

Carini, P. (2001). *Starting strong: A different look at children, schools, and standards*. New York: Teachers College Press.

Clark, C. M. (Ed.). (2001). *Talking shop: Authentic conversation and teacher learning*. New York: Teachers College Press.

Cochran-Smith, M., & Lytle, S. L. (1999). Relationships of knowledge and practice: Teacher learning in communities. *Review of Research in Education, 24*(8), 249–305.

Dewey, J. (1974). Why reflective thinking must be an educational aim. In R. D. Archambault (Ed.), *John Dewey on education: Selected writings* (p. 212). Chicago: University of Chicago Press.

Evans, J. St. B. T. (1989). *Bias in human reasoning*. Hillsdale, NJ: Erlbaum.

Fullan, M. (1993). *Change forces*. London: Falmer Press.

Fullan, M. (1998). The meaning of educational change. In M. Fullan, A. Hargreaves, D. Hopkins, & A. Lieberman (Eds.), *International handbook of educational change* (pp. 214–228). Boston: Kluwer Academic Publishers.

Fullan, M. (1999). *Change forces, the sequel*. Philadelphia: Falmer Press.

Goldman, A. I. (1994). Argument and social epistemology. *Journal of Philosophy, 91*, 27–49.

Habermas, J. (1990). *Moral consciousness and communicative action*. Cambridge, MA: MIT Press.

Hargreaves, A. (1998). The emotions of teaching and educational change. In M. Fullan, A. Hargreaves, D. Hopkins, & A. Lieberman (Eds.), *International handbook of educational change* (pp. 558–575). Boston: Kluwer Academic Publishers.

Hiebert, J., Gallimore, R., & Stigler, J. W. (2002). A knowledge base for the teaching profession: What would it look like and how can we get one? *Educational Researcher, 31*(5), 3–15.

Kasl, E., & Yorks, L. (2002, January 27). An extended epistemology for transformative learning theory and its application through collaborative inquiry. *Teachers College Record*, Article 10878. Available: *http://www.tcrecord.org/Content.asp?ContentID=10878*

Kegan, R., & Lahey, L. L. (2001). *How the way we talk can change the way we work*. San Francisco: Jossey-Bass.

Kim, D. H. (1993). The link between individual and organizational learning. *Sloan Management Review, 35*(1), 37–50.

King, B. M., & Newmann, F. M. (2000). Will teacher learning advance school goals? *Phi Delta Kappan, (81)*8, 576–580.

Kuhn, D. (1991). *The skills of argument*. Cambridge, England: Cambridge University Press.

Lieberman A., & Wood D. R. (2003). *Inside the National Writing Project*. New York: Teachers College Press.

Little, J. W., Gearhart, M., Curry, M., & Kafka, J. (2003). Looking at student work for teacher learning, teacher community, and school reform. *Phi Delta Kappan, 85*(3), 184–192.

McCrary, A. S. (2000). Notes from a marine biologist's daughter: On the arts and science of attention. *Harvard Education Review, 70*, 211–227.

McDonald, J., Mohr, N., Dichter, A., & McDonald, E. (2003). *The power of protocols: An educator's guide to better practice*. New York: Teachers College Press.

McLaughlin, M. W., & Talbert, J. (2001). *Professional communities and the work of high school teaching*. Chicago: University of Chicago Press.

Meier, D. (2002). *In schools we trust: Creating communities of learning in an era of testing and standardization*. Boston: Beacon Press.

Mezirow, J., & Associates. (2001). *Learning as transformation: Critical perspectives on a theory in progress*. San Francisco: Jossey-Bass.

Moshman, D. (1995a). Reasoning as self-constrained thinking. *Human Development, 38*, 53–64.

Moshman, D. (1995b). The construction of moral rationality. *Human Development, 38*, 265–281.

National Research Council. (2000). *How people learn: Brain, mind, experience and school*. J. R. Bransford, A. L. Brown, & R. R. Cocking, Eds., Committee on

Developments in the Science of Learning, Commission on Behavioral and Social Sciences and Education. Washington, DC: National Academy Press.

Newstead, S. E., & Evans, J. St. B. T. (Eds.). (1995). *Perspectives on thinking and reasoning: Essays in honor of Peter Wason.* Hillsdale, NJ: Erlbaum Publishers.

Project Zero, Harvard Graduate School of Education. (2001). *The evidence process: A collaborative approach to understanding and improving teaching and learning.* Cambridge, MA: Author.

Richardson, V. (2003). The dilemmas of professional development. *Phi Delta Kappan, 84*(5), 401–406.

Rodgers, C. R. (2002). Seeing student learning: Teacher change and the role of reflections. *Harvard Educational Review, 72*(2), 230–253.

Salmon, M. H., & Zeitz, C. M. (1995). Analyzing conversational reasoning. *Informal Logic, 17,* 1–23.

Sarason, S. B. (1993). *The predictable failure of educational reform: Can we change course before it's too late?* San Francisco: Jossey-Bass.

Sarason, S. B. (1996). *Revisiting "The culture of the school and the problem of change."* New York: Teachers College Press.

Shapiro, I. (Principal Investigator). (1987). *A private universe* [film]. The Harvard–Smithsonian Center for Astrophysics.

Sparks, D. (2003). [Interview with Michael Fullan: Change agent]. *Journal of Staff Development Council, 24* (1), 55–58.

Smith, F. (1986). *Insult to intelligence: The bureaucratic invasion of our classrooms.* New York: Arbor House.

Stokes, L. (2001). Lessons from an inquiring school: Forms of inquiry and conditions for teacher learning. In A. Lieberman & L. Miller (Eds.), *Teachers caught in the action: Professional development that matters* (pp. 141–158). New York: Teachers College Press.

Youniss, J., & Damon, W. (1992). Social construction in Piaget's theory. In H. Berlin & P. B. Pufal (Eds.), *Piaget's theory: Prospects and possibilities* (pp. 267–286). Hillsdale, NJ: Erlbaum.

Index

About the Authors

David Allen is a researcher at the National Center for Restructuring Education, Schools, and Teaching (NCREST) at Teachers College, Columbia University. He has previously worked at Harvard Project Zero and the Coalition of Essential Schools. He has taught English and ESL at the middle school, high school, and adult levels. In 1996, he received a Fulbright research grant to study school reform in Poland. His publications include: *Assessing Student Learning: From Grading to Understanding* (editor; Teachers College Press, 1998); *Looking Together at Student Work* (co-author; Teachers College Press, 1999); and *The Facilitator's Book of Questions: Tools for Looking Together at Student and Teacher Work* (co-author; Teachers College Press, 2004).

Tina Blythe has been a researcher with Project Zero since 1988. In various research projects she has focused on teaching for understanding, classroom applications of multiple intelligences theory, teacher inquiry groups, and assessment through the collaborative study of student work. A former middle and high school teacher, she currently teaches courses for faculty at the Boston Architectural Center. She has collaborated on a number of books and articles, including *The Teaching for Understanding Guide* (1998); *Looking Together at Student Work* (co-author; Teachers College Press, 1999); and *The Facilitator's Book of Questions: Tools for Looking Together at Student and Teacher Work* (co-author; Teachers College Press, 2004).

Catherine S. Rubin is the president of EduChange, Inc. in New York City. EduChange offers a variety of consultation services to schools and other educational organizations. Before working at EduChange, Ms. Rubin earned her Ed.M. at the Harvard Graduate School of Education. She then worked as a science teacher and administrator in public schools in Boston, San Francisco, and Attleboro, MA. Her recent work focuses on district-wide curriculum articulation, integrated science curriculum development, and teacher-centered school reform efforts.

Steve Seidel is a lecturer on education at the Harvard Graduate School of Education and director of Harvard Project Zero. At Project Zero he is also principal investigator for several projects that examine teachers' reflective practices, the close examination of student work, and documentation of learning. His work and writing for the past decade have largely focused on processes and outcomes of collaborative assessment of student work. Before coming to Project Zero, Mr. Seidel taught theater and language arts in Boston-area high schools for 17 years.

Katherine G. Simon taught high school English and drama before earning her Ph.D. in curriculum and teacher education at Stanford University, where she also taught and supervised student teachers in the Stanford Teacher Education Program. After several years of developing professional development initiatives and directing research at the Coalition of Essential Schools, Dr. Simon is currently co-Executive Director of that organization. Her book, *Moral Questions in the Classroom: How to Get Kids to Think Deeply About Real Life and Their School Work* (2001), was named "Outstanding Book in Curriculum for 2001–2002" by the American Educational Research Association.

Alexandra T. Weinbaum co-directs the Academy for Educational Development's (AED's) Center for School and Community Services. Before assuming this position, Ms. Weinbaum developed curricula on women's studies for the high school classroom and worked in school districts in New York City as director of sex, race, and national origins desegregation initiatives. For the last 15 years her work at AED has focused on school improvement, especially in low-income communities. She currently directs projects that promote school-wide inquiry into teaching and learning and is the principal author of a number of studies and evaluations of school improvement initiatives and youth development programs. She holds a Ph.D. in history from Columbia University.